Cultural Studies in Foreign Language Education

Multilingual Matters

Please contact us for the latest book information:
Multilingual Matters, Bank House, 8a Hill Rd,
Clevedon, Avon BS21 7HH, England

MULTILINGUAL MATTERS 46
Series Editor: Derrick Sharp

Cultural Studies in Foreign Language Education

Michael Byram

MULTILINGUAL MATTERS LTD
Clevedon • Philadelphia

For: Marie Thérèse, Alice, Ian

Library of Congress Cataloging in Publication Data

Byram, Michael.
  Cultural studies in foreign language education/Michael Byram.
    p. cm.—(Multilingual matters ; 46)
  Bibliography: p.
  Includes index.
  1. Language and languages—Study and teaching (Secondary) 2. Area
studies. I. Title. II. Series.
P53.B94 1988
418'.007'12—dc19

British Library Cataloguing in Publication Data

Byram, Michael
  Cultural studies in foreign language
  education—(Multilingual matters ; 46).
  1. Foreign languages. Teaching. Implications
  of cultural differences
  I. Title
  418'.007

  ISBN 1-85359-018-5
  ISBN 1-85359-017-7 Pbk

Multilingual Matters Ltd

Bank House, 8a Hill Road   &   242 Cherry Street
Clevedon, Avon BS21 7HH   Philadelphia, PA 19106–1906
England   USA

Copyright © 1989 Michael Byram

Cover design by Jussi Nurmi
Index compiled by Meg Davies
Typeset by Mathematical Composition Setters Ltd, Salisbury, Wiltshire
Printed and bound in Great Britain by WBC Print Ltd

Contents

Preface

The pages which follow have two distinct functions. They encapsulate my thoughts about foreign language teaching as they have developed in the last decade and more whilst I have been teaching French and German to English comprehensive school pupils and subsequently training others to do so. In this respect these pages are retrospective and reflect my dissatisfaction with some changes in emphasis in foreign language teaching in what have nonetheless been twenty years of genuine progress. Foreign language teaching is, both in my experience as learner and teacher and in my pedagogic philosophy, as education, an emancipation from the confines of one's native habitat and culture; the current emphasis on language teaching as skill training is apt to lose that from sight.

This book is also exploratory and prospective. It includes some of my efforts to clarify how the educational value of foreign language teaching can be made more available and accessible to learners and teachers alike. It explores some theoretical avenues and reports some empirical investigation of how learners can be given the opportunity and encouragement to escape from their own habitat and culture, however briefly and in full acceptance that they will return to it—but with a new perception of it and themselves. For the cultural emancipation of language learning is an experience whose complexity is far from exhausted by reference to grammar, semantics, visits to foreign countries, reading foreign literature, studying foreign political systems, social issues and historical events. It is all these intellectual endeavours and much more. It is the emotional experience of abandoning one's language in the first few lessons of foreign language learning, of saying goodbye to home and country on the first visit abroad, of becoming enamoured of exotic places, food, people—and perhaps one special person —however near or distant the destination might be from one's native frontiers. I believe that insufficient attention is paid by teachers and researchers to all of this and have written this book as part of my efforts to examine foreign language learning as education in its many-faceted complexity.

The book has been written contemporaneously and, in many of its aspects, integrally with an empirical research project financed by the Economic and Social Research Council. One chapter is written jointly with two of my colleagues on that project, Dr Veronica Esarte-Sarries and Ms Susan Taylor, who have both contributed more to this book than the chapter which bears their names; I am grateful to them both for listening and commenting in many conversations. The project, 'The effects of language teaching on young people's perceptions of other cultures', was planned by Dr Patricia Allatt and myself. To Dr Allatt, who worked on the project for one year full-time and as consultant for the following two years, I owe a great debt of intellectual gratitude.

In addition to this theoretical and empirical work within our national and regional confines, I believe that work on language learning should itself break through the paradoxical tendency of language teachers and researchers—particularly in Britain—to concern themselves only with their own national scene. To this end I have sought to establish co-operative work with other researchers in Western Europe, initially through an international symposium on cultural studies in language teaching in Durham in 1986 (financed by the Economic and Social Research Council and the Deutsche Forschungsgesellschaft). Through this I have of course benefited intellectually and personally and owe much to all the members of that symposium, but particularly to Dieter Buttjes who was joint organiser. The papers from that symposium are part of the context for this book. A final piece in the contextual jigsaw is an as yet pilot project of research into the experience of residence abroad for university-level students of foreign languages. These are the most advanced learners for whom the emancipatory value of language learning might be supposed most developed and complex. Residence abroad as part of their study—in the vast majority of cases an obligatory part of their course—might be assumed to be the apogee of that education, which many will pass on to other learners when they themselves become teachers. This research is being carried out by Dr Geof Alred and myself at Durham University.

With all this I want simply to say that a complex issue demands complex investigation and the following pages are simply one aspect to be seen in a larger context.

No book is written without a secretary, an editor and a publisher. All three—Mrs Doreen Wilson, Mr Derrick Sharp and Mr Mike Grover—have contributed not only their professional expertise but also their personal interest, and I am particularly grateful to my editor and publisher for accepting a manuscript which treads none of the beaten tracks of language teaching literature.

No book is written without its being an expression of the writer's self, whether it be an academic thesis or a collection of lyric poetry. This one is no exception. The reader will guess that my concern with foreign language learning as education reflects my own education in school, college, among friends in foreign countries and in my own bilingual family. The journey from a council estate in Dewsbury to the university in Durham was further than the 100 miles which separate them.

Michael Byram
Cosse en Champagne
Summer, 1987

Acknowledgements

Earlier versions of parts of this book have been published elsewhere:

— Chapter 1 in *Sacred Cows in Education*, 1983, edited by Frank Coffield and Richard Goodings, Edinburgh University Press.
— Chapter 2 in *Journal of Curriculum Studies*, 1988, edited by David Hamilton, Taylor and Francis Ltd.
— Chapter 4 in *Language Teaching*, 1986, edited by Valerie Kinsella, Cambridge University Press.

I am grateful to the above for permission to use the material in its revised form.

Introduction

This is a book written by a language teacher for language teachers about the hidden curriculum of foreign language (FL) teaching. I refer to that part of foreign language teaching which conveys information, attitudes, images and perhaps even prejudice about the people and countries where the particular language is spoken. It is a book which arises from my experience of FL teaching in Britain, but I also know that the issues to be raised are important in foreign language teaching in Europe and North America, and perhaps even further afield. It is also a book which draws on the disciplines which surround language teaching, pursuing the applications of psychology, anthropology and others as they seem appropriate to someone who is a specialist in none of them, writing for other non-specialists. There are in this approach the advantages of drawing out those ideas which are really appropriate instead of having ideas thrust upon us by those who do not teach languages. There are also the disadvantages of venturing into a specialist field without due training. Whether the trade-off has been a profitable one has to be decided by my readers, specialists and non-specialists alike, language teachers and those others who may happen to open these pages.

I would wish to make it clear from the beginning that I am writing about *foreign* language teaching, by which I refer to language teaching, e.g. French, in classrooms situated in a different linguistic environment, e.g. a Danish *folkeskole*, as part of the learner's general education. I would contrast this with *second* language teaching, taking place within a target language environment, e.g. children of immigrant workers learning German in a West German *Grundschule*. This is a working distinction which serves to delineate the area of interest, rather than a theoretical statement. There will be points in my argument which could refer without that distinction to many language teaching situations, but for the sake of clarity I shall concentrate on foreign language teaching and leave readers to make other connections as they think appropriate.

I have already mentioned the context for foreign language teaching with which I am most concerned: 'general education'. I am concerned above all with the work of the foreign language teacher in ordinary—usually 'secondary'—schools throughout the Western world. Their pupils come to school because schooling is obligatory, and they learn a foreign language because it is a part of the curriculum deemed by educationists to be a 'normal' part of general education. The justifications and explanations offered for foreign language teaching are varied, and to some extent influenced by the educational philosophy and traditions of particular countries or by the position of the national language on the international linguistic market place. For example, there may be a 'vocational' or a 'national interest' element introduced, just as a vocational justification or national interest is used to encourage pupils to learn some other school subjects, such as the natural sciences. For the teacher and learner involved day by day in the business of the foreign language classroom, however, long-term goals and comparisons with skills-learning for a particular career are not terribly relevant. It is with the everyday business of foreign language teaching and learning in the ordinary classroom that I am concerned when discussing how, what and why people learn about other countries, other peoples, other ways of life while they are learning a foreign language.

The purpose of each of the following chapters is then to take an aspect of what I shall call Cultural Studies and to examine its theoretical and practical dimensions. In some ways this is premature because I am not in a position to offer a model or theory of Cultural Studies in anything approaching a complete form. And yet it is proper and necessary that language teachers should think about Cultural Studies in more than haphazard and intuitive ways. For most teachers already have their own intuitive and practice-influenced theories and their practices are already part of foreign language teaching, without any guarantee that their practices will stand up to critical enquiry. There is no guarantee that their practices are leading to the results which they aim for, results which have been determined on intuitive grounds. Therefore much of the following discussion will be concerned with examining current practice, as well as with the theoretical bases on which sound practice might in future be based. Moreover, despite my suggestion that we are still in the early stages of theoretical discussion of Cultural Studies, there is nonetheless a well developed literature on the question of teaching about the country, culture or civilisation associated with a language. Unfortunately it is not very influential in practice, because the teachers involved are *language* teachers. Since their major concern is with language, they see the rest as 'background' or 'context' which has a low priority in their concerns and stimulates little thought about aims, methods, evaluation, assessment and all the things which are discussed at length with respect to *language* teaching. Such a generalisation is, of course, open to many exceptions. Let me simply say it is a generalisation from my own experience and observations of others. Essentially, therefore, this book is an attempt to share my efforts to think about practice with those who believe that practice does not and cannot in fact exist without theory.

After this initial statement of intent and first attempt to clarify the extent of the subject under discussion, the rest of this introductory chapter offers a framework for discussing current practice and developing future practice and theory together. It is the framework on which the following chapters are founded.

First of all, let me say more precisely what I include under the label 'Cultural Studies'. Every foreign language lesson includes some spoken or written text and usually some visual image which refer to a particular foreign way of life. The reference may be ignored by teacher and learner, as they attempt to describe their own world using the foreign language—for example using 'le pain' to refer to an English loaf of bread, but the implicit reference, to a French baguette, cannot be avoided. Some foreign language lessons include description of a scene in the foreign country in which the text might figure. Some lessons include discussion and even evaluation of the way of life in the foreign country as an activity worthwhile in itself. (There are even, in British schools, some lessons labelled French or German Studies in which no foreign language is taught and only the way of life of the country or countries is the object of the lesson.) Thus under the term 'Cultural Studies' I refer to any information, knowledge or attitudes about the foreign culture which is evident during foreign language teaching. 'Cultural Studies' is taught and learnt both overtly and implicitly, both consciously and incidentally, in much the same way as other components of the overt and hidden curriculum, and thus merits thorough discussion in curricular terms. It is an important feature of the viewpoint taken here that Cultural Studies should not be considered merely as incidental to the 'real business' of language teaching. To discuss its significance as part of the general education curriculum from this basis is therefore to venture a step beyond the dominant philosophy in much foreign language teaching.

The first stage of my argument will seek to establish that Cultural Studies has a rightful place as part of language teaching, not just as an adjunct to language learning, not just as a means of creating better communication but as an integral component with appropriate aims and methods. It certainly plays a role in *language* teaching in the sense that words in the foreign language refer to meanings in a particular culture creating a semantic relationship which the learner needs to comprehend. Yet, where language teaching is part of general education, there is much more to it than this. Language learning, it is often said, 'broadens the horizons' and, if it does, then it has educational significance. In fact what is really meant is that cultural learning, as a result of language learning, broadens the horizons, and once that is recognised then the need for good 'culture teaching' becomes quite evident. (It is not my intention in this introduction to develop this, or other points, in great depth. They will be taken up in subsequent chapters.) Given this basic position the need for systematic and rigorous analysis of Cultural Studies becomes clear. What I am seeking is an adequate didactic of Cultural Studies, and what I propose next is an outline of how such a didactic may be developed.

There are a number of avenues of worthwhile enquiry which lead in different directions. Some may turn out to be without issue, others may join up at some point in the future and yet others may lead to completely new vistas and thus to re-definitions of purposes. It is important to investigate them all without requiring them at this stage to lead to mutually coherent or related results. For example, there is the avenue which sets out from within current practice and theory in language teaching. It is, however, also possible to start from within another discipline, social anthropology. It is equally necessary to investigate cultural learning from a psychological point of view. Each of these, and others, must be considered both on the basis of empirical research of current practices and with the help of the theory available within established disciplines. Here, I shall describe briefly a number of areas of enquiry and indicate how certain avenues of investigation might be expected to throw light on them.

Starting from the position that Cultural Studies is an integral part of foreign language teaching, it is necessary to consider its precise relationship to the 'subject' and to secondary education as a whole. It is not enough simply to assume that Cultural Studies as a natural part of language teaching will inevitably lead to positive educational outcomes. *The educational value of Cultural Studies within language teaching and within the secondary school curriculum as a whole is the first area of enquiry*. It is necessary to approach it from the point of view of curriculum theory: how it relates to the principles on which curricula are developed. It is also necessary to consider the relationship between language and culture, and here we may look to work in anthropology and philosophy as well as the more frequently consulted disciplines of psychology and linguistics.

Cultural Studies is a pedagogical activity, and it will also be necessary to consider the processes of teaching and learning which might and already do take place and what learning outcomes are to be expected. Clearly the latter are the realisation of the purposes and aims identified in curricular and educational terms, and the links with the first area of enquiry must be kept in mind. The question of pedagogical structuring raises other issues too. First, there is the need to identify a body of knowledge and also a form of knowledge on which to develop that which is peculiar to Cultural Studies as a school subject. These must, however, be seen in their relationship to *language* learning. They must be equally related to the psychological processes and outcomes and to the definition of the concept of culture and of the particular culture to be taught. To start from a form of knowledge is also to imply a particular approach to curriculum development. These interrelationships can be summarised as a second area of enquiry: *to structure Cultural Studies in a pedagogical manner which takes account of ways of structuring our knowledge of the world and in particular of other cultures, which is influenced by knowledge of cognitive and affective learning processes and which can be expected to lead to specific psychological outcomes: the pedagogy of Cultural Studies must also be related to other aspects of foreign language learning.* The disciplines which are already concerned with our ways of knowing about other cultures are social anthropology and cross-cultural psychology, and in addition it is likely that the psychology of cultural cognition in the native culture will throw light on the psychology of experience from exposure to other cultures. Thus a theory of cultural learning within foreign language teaching will have to take account of the psychology of cultural or ethnic identity and its relationship to the psychological processes which may be developed as a result of learning a foreign language and culture. Such learning will typically include classroom experience and an occasional sojourn in the target culture.

The area of pedagogical structuring is closely connected with a third area of enquiry: the methodology of cultural teaching. This is an area which is particularly open to empirical investigation of current practices. Such practices are perhaps mainly constructed on intuitive theories of cultural learning and generalised educational aims of social learning and 'broadening pupils' horizons'. Such theories and generalisations are likely to be intuitive and tacit because of the lack of teacher training for cultural studies. Nonetheless the practices which are handed down are worthy of investigation in order both to establish the effects of particular techniques and to clarify the basis on which future curricular change has to be founded. A methodology of cultural teaching must also take account of theoretical discussion of educational aims, concepts of culture and cultural learning and of pedagogical structuring. A methodology should ultimately be developed from a psychological theory which in turn takes account of the educational context. From such a methodology there will follow a number of methods or techniques and here again empirical research will reveal current practices and their consequences. Thus the third area includes both *the methodology and techniques of Cultural Studies teaching.* I shall in fact argue later that the questions of subject content—what is likely to be taught about a particular culture—and of teaching methods can be linked. The difficult problem of describing and selecting from a particular culture may be solved by concentrating rather on teaching 'ways of knowing' about culture, and the experience of cultural identity in the complex and structured practices of daily life.

Finally, we come to issues of assessment and evaluation. All teachers want to know whether their teaching is effective, and assessment of pupils' or students' learning is one indicator of this. Unfortunately, assessment in the form of examination has frequently been interpreted rather as an indicator of students' capacity to learn than of teachers' capacity to teach, but it is with the issue of teaching efficacy that I am concerned here. A related issue is whether the teaching and learning process in a given situation is in fact an adequate realisation of the underlying aims and principles. Evaluation of teaching programmes has become a highly developed occupation within education and any attempt to refine Cultural Studies must take this into account. Although pupil/student assessment in a narrow sense, focused on individuals' attainment, should logically follow the determination of aims and processes, it should nonetheless be considered in concurrent evaluation developed alongside the process of determining aims, psychological theory, materials and methodology. Thus a fourth area of enquiry, *evaluation of Cultural Studies teaching and assessment of learning*, needs to be investigated simultaneously with the other three. In addition to established work in educational evaluation, there is a tradition of assessment not only in language teaching but also in other curriculum subjects which may be related, for example in History and English as Mother Tongue. Moreover, if we are to assess both cognitive and affective aspects of cultural learning, then work in cross-cultural psychology on the effects of exposure to other cultures may be significant.

The framework proposed above might appear too complex or ambitious for an aspect of education which is only part of a school subject; a part, moreover, which is usually accorded little importance if it is considered at all. It might appear, particularly to secondary school teachers, that I am elevating Cultural Studies to the status of a separate subject when it is best left to the intuitions of the teachers themselves. My response would be that a significant part of the educational value of foreign language teaching derives from Cultural Studies and that the intuitions of many foreign language teachers—trained through the study of literature and linguistics—are unrefined by those academic disciplines which are the most appropriate support for Cultural Studies. It may well be—and empirical research will be discussed later—that the effects of foreign language teaching on young people's perceptions of other cultures are not as positive and accurate as the language teaching profession has always taken for granted. I believe that there is sufficient need to examine Cultural Studies in its own right, while bearing in mind that language and culture are so interlinked that it is within foreign language teaching that Cultural Studies must surely continue to be taught. As for the complexity and ambition of the framework it can only be said that the whole education process, understood as the enculturation of children into the society in which they live, is complex and ambitious and that living in any Western society involves contact with many cultures within and outside it. In a more restricted sense, Cultural Studies, viewed as the learning and acquisition of a culture, albeit foreign, is a microcosm of the larger education process and needs to be treated with the complexity, ambition and seriousness which we accord to the whole. This book is written in that spirit. It is an attempt to introduce the issues which underlie current practice. It draws on the relatively limited literature available from within language teaching. It explores some of the avenues indicated above and engages aspects of the areas of enquiry designated in the framework. It will nonetheless be evident that there is no claim of comprehensive coverage in the following pages, still less of providing all the answers, or even of asking all the appropriate questions. The four areas of enquiry designated above are not all dealt with equally and not always directly in the terms used in this introduction. Where possible, links will be made and relationships investigated, but if there is one single purpose to this book it is not to provide a complete and neat account of a closely defined issue but rather to essay a number of independent approaches to an important and complex topic.

1 Foreign Language Teaching and Education

Foreign language competence has since ancient times been a sign of 'the educated man', and it is not necessary to seek beyond the 'man in the street' to find evidence of admiration for and acceptance of the principle that being educated includes being able to 'speak' a foreign language. What precisely is meant by 'speak', what the nature of the competence might be is, however, a much more difficult issue. There are in the contemporary world millions of people who speak more than one language but who would be considered uneducated by the European 'man in the street'. The man in the street of many European countries is furthermore himself able to 'speak' a foreign language but would not consider himself educated because of it. It is a complex business which includes factors such as the status of the language in question, the degree of literacy in the language, the uses to which the competence is put, the origin of the competence in school or elsewhere, diplomatic relations and political climate, immigration laws and economic development; that is, factors which go far beyond the linguistic and scholastic.

Thus when justifications are advanced for the inclusion of foreign language teaching in schools there is a tendency to include reasons which go beyond some unclear notion of mere linguistic competence. There is the feeling that education is not complete without a foreign language. This has become all the more evident in the contemporary world as curricula are re-assessed in the light of the 'knowledge explosion' to which we have become particularly sensitive in the twentieth century, and secondly as a result of the extension of schooling to people other than the aristocratic and ruling classes. When 'new' subjects begin to demand a place in the curriculum—whether computer studies or woodwork and cookery—the 'old' subjects have to begin to defend and explain their presence; here is one example:

A l'interieur de la scolarité obligatoire, l'enseignement des langues doit être repensé, dans sa specificité propre et en liaison avec l'ensemble des disciplines (reflexion sur le langage, en liaison avec la langue maternelle et les mathematiques, développement de l'expression personelle en liaison avec les enseignements litteraires et artistiques, ouverture sur le monde en liaison avec l'histoire, la géographie, l'économie, les sciences . . .)
(Charte des Langues Vivantes, 1980: 313)

What is here sought in co-operation with other subjects, an additional role to the instilling of linguistic competence, is elsewhere claimed independently for foreign language teaching (H.M.I., 1985: para. 52):

Foreign language study expands the linguistic area of experience by affording interesting linguistic comparisons. It also offers insight into another culture and as such is concerned with the human and social area of experience. Throughout the course pupils can be encouraged to view the familiar from a different angle, not least in terms of people's behaviour, and thereby widen horizons and break down feelings of insularity.

These kinds of account[1] appear to be quite consonant with the notion of being educated. Why then the need to make policy statements, to define aims and goals? Is it simply a matter of staving off attacks from new subjects or is there something significant in the emphasis on '*re*pensé'? The Charte des Langues Vivantes identifies the right to 'cette formation indispensable dans le monde actuel que constitue l'apprentissage des langues et l'ouverture aux cultures étrangères et d'acquèrir les outils linguistiques nécessaires à leur activité professionelle' and suggests that these two objectives are not incompatible. The charter also criticises the approach to second language teaching for immigrant children which has been encouraged by the French education authorities (p. 312):

En laissant croire que l'apprentissage d'une langue peut se limiter à l'acquisition d'un outil de communication minimale, les pouvoirs publics ont fait disparaître aux yeux de l'ensemble des parents, des élèves et des enseignants, le rôle que l'apprentissage devrait jouer dans la formation de la personnalité.

There is here an evident unease about the potential separation of two facets of language teaching: the instilling of a useful skill and the encouraging of an open attitude and understanding of other cultures. The claim that they are quite compatible is no doubt justified but the vigour with which it is made betrays fears which are not unfounded. In order to understand this situation, let us return to the origins of 'modern' language teaching in the nineteenth century, where the tensions between the aims and methodologies of ancient (classics) and modern language teaching were not unlike the tensions within foreign language teaching today.

In broad terms there have been two opposing tendencies in 'modern' language teaching since it was grafted onto 'classical' language teaching in the nineteenth century. The *anciens* of the nineteenth century wanted to model their teaching of modern languages, usually French,[2] directly on the teaching of Latin and Greek (Gilbert, 1953–5). The consequent 'grammar-translation method' has been widely and justly criticised, but it should not be criticised for not doing what it did not set out to do: to produce speakers of the language on the model of, and assessed against the ideal of, a native speaker—and a highly educated native speaker to boot. It is more reasonable to assume that it set out to produce a 'native reader and writer'—a more manageable and attainable aim, I would suggest, whatever the method. To produce the native-like speaker has, however, been the implied aim of other methods proposed by the *modernes* and dominating the field each in turn since the late nineteenth century. Although the argument has throughout that period focused largely on methods, the underlying but unspoken debate has been about aims. The result has been that, with the exception of the early days when the *modernes* had to argue their case on the home ground of the *anciens*, the *anciens* have had to argue the case for their method as if they aimed at producing native speaker substitutes. At both periods the differences in aims were obscured beneath the arguments about methods. One might think, in times when 'notions' and 'functions' abound, that all that is past. Yet in the advanced classes of secondary schools and the language classes of universities in Britain, the influence of 'grammar-translation' is still strong. There are indications that new examinations may encourage changes in methods, but it remains to be seen how long this takes.

In other, earlier stages of language learning in British schools—and in some countries throughout the language learning process—'communicative language teaching' is making a major impact. This is the most obvious indication of a triumph for the *modernes*, since the language teaching profession is thereby in all essentials committed to a view of language as communication. 'Communicative competence' is the aim for all pupils, but in different ways and with different degrees of accuracy according to the ability of the learner. Yet in Britain, and perhaps elsewhere, one of the reasons for the acceptance of anything 'communicative'—be it method, aim, material, psychology or whatever—has been that is is seen as a better means of motivating pupils, of providing 'relevant' teaching. 'Relevance' is interpreted as 'relevant to the needs of the pupil' and a needs analysis of pupils' present or postulated future communication requirements is used as a basis for developing a language teaching syllabus. In this process needs are selected which the pupils can appreciate on a commonsense view of language: that it is a means of passing messages between people. The problem is that pupils may have needs which are not apparent or comprehensible to them but which those professionally engaged in education can see and ought to fulfil. The danger is that teachers themselves are so accustomed to using the commonsense arguments of relevance and usefulness of foreign language teaching in fulfilling the putative communication needs of pupils, that they relegate other educational needs to a second rank—or even forget them. This is not to dismiss needs analysis, especially as developed in work for the Council of Europe. Nor is it to suggest that needs analysis as developed for adult language learners is of no account in dealing with children. It is simply to remind us that there are other needs which must not be forgotten, arising from the fact that we are teaching children and contributing to their education. The Council of Europe work itself does not ignore general educational aims (Trim, 1980: 10), but the thrust of communicative language teaching is so strong that such aims are likely to be forgotten in the routine of the classroom.

Furthermore, the problem of the realism of the needs remains. If we justify language teaching—and motivate pupils—solely, or even just mainly, by putative communication needs and those needs turn out to be non-existent, then the justification disappears—and most of the motivation with it. When we attempt to persuade pupils by this appeal to relevance and appropriateness, and they argue that they do not and will not have such communicative needs—or, what has the same effect, cannot imagine themselves having such needs—then we are pre-programming our work for failure in their eyes. This is bad enough, but when the teachers themselves are persuaded that this is the main justification and then cannot continue to believe in it, they too are programmed for failure. In addition to this, the unattainable and insidious ideal of imitating and evaluating communicative performance by comparison with the native speaker and writer can undermine the confidence of pupil and teacher alike. The philosophy that language teaching aims to prepare pupils for future communication can lead the teacher to a desperate pass, as might be observed in countless classrooms throughout secondary schools in Britain, or collèges in France (Weil, 1982). Even the countries noted for their language learning, for example Denmark (Byram, 1982), do not escape the danger of in-built failure.

Let us therefore retrace a few steps and take another look at the notion of needs. We must look at the education of pupils, at their needs as the teacher perceives them, at the contribution to their whole educational development that language teaching can offer. When questions are put in these terms, most language teachers will find answers, and indeed such answers have been articulated in the English 'National Criteria' for the General Certificate of Secondary Education: French, where it is implicitly claimed that such a contribution is not incompatible with the approach through communicative needs. The document sets out the 'educational purposes of following a course in French for the GCSE examination'. Seven aims are specified, although it is argued that some of them 'cannot readily be assessed for examination purposes'. The aims can be grouped into four rough categories although they appear in an arbitrary order in the document. The first group might be entitled 'communication', including aims 1 and 2:

> to develop the ability to use French effectively for purposes of practical communication
>
> to form a sound base of the skills, language and attitudes required for further study, work and leisure.

A second category involves only one of the aims and could be called 'education about language' or 'language awareness':

> to develop an awareness of the nature of language and language learning.

A third category, central to the present discussion, could be entitled 'Cultural awareness' and includes aims 3 and 6:

> to offer insights into the culture and civilisation of French-speaking countries
>
> to encourage positive attitudes to foreign language learning and to speakers of foreign languages and a sympathetic approach to other cultures and civilisations.

These three categories are specific to foreign language teaching, or at least central to it in ways not found in other subjects. The final category is of aims 5 and 7 which are shared by many other areas of the curriculum:

> to provide enjoyment and intellectual stimulation
>
> to promote learning skills of a more general application (e.g. analysis, memorising, drawing of inferences).
> (D.E.S. and Welsh Office, 1985: 1)

Unfortunately, having stated that such broader aims may not all be examinable, the document proceeds without more ado to determine objectives and means of examining which relate in any substantial way only to the first aim. Clearly in our present state of knowledge of assessment, we are more able to measure skills and knowledge on the one hand, than changes in attitudes and insight on the other. If this leads to neglect of the latter then the fears of the writers of 'La Charte des Langues Vivantes' are clearly justified. The development of pupils' personality, their capacity for empathy, their understanding of others' experience, emotions and rationality are in great danger of being ignored. Even if the only consideration were efficiency in communication, it is evident that all this has to be included in language teaching which aims to instil an ability to communicate with people from other cultures at anything beyond an elementary and extremely basic level. If language teaching is to claim a genuine contribution to pupils' education as citizens of mature civilisations, the focus should shift towards rather than away from assessment of pupils' changes in attitude and insight into other cultures, and their own.

This point of view, however, is not synonymous with rejecting the notion of teaching for communication. Although it is not in itself sufficient justification for foreign language teaching, I do not propose that we reject the methods recently developed for teaching pupils to communicate, although I share Trim's (1983) doubts about the widely held view that communication simply means the passing of messages. Yet my justification for teaching pupils to communicate in a foreign language differs from the 'utilitarian' arguments which promise some future profitable application for languages. First, it is the nature of language that its prime, though not sole, function is interpersonal communication, usually in the form of speech. Yet the language of the classroom is 'rehearsal' language (Hawkins, 1981: 240–75; Mitchell, Parkinson & Johnstone, 1981: 66) which does not even have the force of communicating information in the way that children's make-believe does. Young children playing at doctors and nurses, teacher and pupils and so on, are involved in creative make-believe: each actor is ignorant of what the others will say and has to react spontaneously to their speech. Classroom role-playing in the foreign language which does not have this element of the unknown does not contain this creativity. In this respect, the essence of language is misrepresented and the pupils are ill-served. They are not properly equipped for their projected needs, even if these are realistic, for in the classroom they do not meet the inevitable requirements of creativity and spontaneity which reality demands of them. Fortunately there is some evidence that British teachers are developing techniques which demand creative performance and response to new and unexpected experience.

Where that full experience of communication in a foreign language really does take place, then it is an aspect of a pupil's development which is unique to language teaching. For the first time pupils experience the world without their mother tongue, perhaps struggling to handle the world and their experience of it, perhaps even retreating from exposure to experience without the security of a means of containing and controlling it, but nonetheless discovering that there is a Pandora's Box whose existence they had hitherto not suspected. Such experience constitutes a step towards acquiring the flexibility of mind, the independence of attachment to a single language which the natural bilingual often has. This 'bilingual vision' (Byram, 1981) potentially enables pupils to acquire a greater depth of vision of the world, another dimension of experience, which seeing through two languages appears to create (Lambert, 1978; Hamers & Blanc, 1983: 91–7). Valuable as this insight into the nature of bilingual vision may be, sheer experience of communication in another language for the non-natural, partial bilingual nurtured in the classroom is not enough. The amount of that experience can only be minuscule compared to mother-tongue experience, and by the time foreign language learning begins in the secondary school pupils are so constrained by their own language that they need active help to evaluate the experience and to take an outsider's view of the mother tongue. It is such evaluation and contemplation from outside which are a normal, almost unconscious part of daily experience for the natural bilingual. To provide help of this kind would clearly have consequences for the methods and activities of language teaching, which cannot be considered in detail here but which have been developed in Britain as 'Language Awareness' (cf. Donmall, 1985; Hawkins, 1987). Given such methodological changes, the ability to communicate in a foreign language is not merely potentially useful, but also a unique dimension of a child's development.

Another of the aims quoted from the criteria for English examinations is closely connected with this issue of looking at language as part of the process of learning. To acquire 'insight' into language learning is, at first sight, simply a useful skill, the skill of learning other languages which in turn will be useful. Indeed this can answer the argument that language needs cannot be foreseen, for adults who have learnt one language at school will be better equipped to learn another which may become necessary for them later. This is intuitively true and anyone who has taught adults and distinguished the *vrais débutants* from the *faux débutants* will agree, although there is no empirical research to sustain this claim (Sidwell, 1984).

Yet what of the many adults who will never require an additional language for professional or other purposes? If it were only a question of acquiring the skill of learning languages, then there would be 'only' the satisfaction of the craftsman—the satisfaction which some people seek in adult education classes, choosing to learn a language where they might just as easily have chosen to learn carpentry. There is no inherent reason why this sort of satisfaction should be accessible only to adults; we ought perhaps to help pupils to see this rather than leaving them to work it out for themselves. Yet it is surely the case that to know about language learning is to know about language. Moreover, those who are helped to see that they know about language learning—whether adults or children—are also helped to realise that they know about language. The connection with the notion of 'bilingual vision' lies in the fact that in both cases there is an increase in pupils' understanding of language, of their 'awareness of language' (Hawkins, 1987), which in turn enhances pupils' knowledge of themselves, of their relation to others and of their knowledge of the world. The educational value of this is too obvious to need further emphasis.

Two others, numbers 3 and 6, of the quoted aims bring us nearer to our central theme: that the educational value of teaching about other cultures is no less self-evident. Let it be said immediately that by 'culture and civilisation' I refer to the whole way of life of the foreign country, including but not limited to its production in the arts, philosophy and 'high culture' in general; the issue will be discussed in more detail in Chapter 5. It is not evident that language teachers and the writers of the aims quoted above also take this view, but I shall make this assumption for the moment.

The contribution which the understanding of another culture and civilisation should make to the reduction of prejudice and the encouragement of tolerance is one of the unchallenged beliefs of language teachers. It ought therefore to surprise us how little status 'background studies', 'Landeskunde' or 'civilisation' have; but the English term is in fact symptomatic. The induction of pupils in Western countries into the international and intercultural dimensions of their society could be furthered by direct experience of a foreign culture which is uniquely available through the language. Yet language teachers seem to accord little value to cultural studies. In Britain many of them have been trained in this belief by university departments of French or German etc., which ought more properly to be called departments of French or German (etc.) literature. In this tradition they will argue that civilisation or Landeskunde need not be taught directly, that it will be a corollary of language or literature teaching. In other European countries the situation is not so dire, but despite the well established tradition of teaching Landeskunde in

Germany the practices to be observed in schools and universities are still open to criticism (Buttjes, 1982). There is then a serious claim to contribute to pupils' personal development and general education but thus far it has not been taken seriously by the language teaching profession, let alone other educators, as Goodson & McGivney also conclude after surveying the role of modern languages in promoting knowledge of Europe in general (1985: 121–31). It is too readily assumed that exposure to *language* teaching will lead to some kind of cultural learning.

This can lead to problems. For example, if cultural knowledge is to be passed to pupils incidentally, teachers ought to be aware of the representation of the foreign culture which they and their course books offer for acquisition:

The learner is presented with a picture of a France populated by unworried and friendly middle-class people; they have no economic problems, no housing problems. The learner does not see the French at work: shopping and spare-time occupations preponderate. In all the textbooks the relationships between the persons are very friendly, almost idyllic; there is no generation gap, no conflicts. There are no social or political problems; there are no blacks, no Arabs, no immigrant workers, no unemployment, no minority groups of any kind. To sum up, all the language course material gives a socially and ideologically one-sided picture of France and the French.
(Risager & Andersen, 1978: my translation)

This account of beginners' course books could well describe many British courses and—*mutatis mutandis*—many English courses in Germany (Byram & Schilder, 1986). The fact that it is a description of Danish books simply underlines the importance of the point. The Danish, British and, doubtless, German and other views of France and the French presented to future Europeans is distorted. The distortion is then increased by exaggeration of the typical, by concentration on the differences between the foreign and home cultures, so that the stereotype Frenchman hovers in the background and dominates the impression pupils take away with them, despite the best efforts of the teacher. Eventually, those who go on to further study will probably come across the minorities Risager and Andersen mention. Yet it is only a proportion who reach this stage and even they see France through the funnel of extracts from intellectually respectable and not necessarily representative newspapers and magazines (Mariet, 1985), rather than through the experience of individuals for whom they might find some empathy. They too remember as much, and perhaps more vividly, the characters and world of their first, formative years of learning

French—more than they remember or are impressed by the intellectual displays of complex articles from *Le Nouvel Observateur* or *Le Monde*.

Empathy is as important as the degree of realism in the picture of France. Even if it is argued that the 'special' problems of minorities should not dominate the world of French family life presented to young learners, there remains the problem of empathy. Risager and Andersen point out that relations between characters are friendly, free of conflict and almost idyllic. Textbook writers who think that pupils live in something like the Enid Blyton world of textbook families are deluding themselves. Even as a fantasy fiction, such a world has little attraction for the age group beginning French, and it is in fact intended to be realist fiction. For many adolescents life in and about their own family is in no way idyllic. How then can they be expected to take this textbook world seriously? On the other hand, current research[3] indicates that some pupils learning French from textbooks dispensing with the textbook family feel they are missing an important dimension. They want to know about family life, and not just learn how to 'survive' as a tourist in France. We need to find a means of representing the way of life which avoids the pitfalls of family idyll and of superficial tourism.

In short, complacency about the inevitable beneficial effects on attitudes produced in the course of language teaching is ill-judged. There are good reasons for stressing that language is above all a means of communication, for intending that knowledge of language learning and of language will be part of what the learners take away from their course in a particular language, for believing that positive attitudes towards other peoples and cultures might come from a close understanding of one of them. Yet, none of these can be taken for granted. They all have to be pursued with time and energy, which at the moment tend to be wholly devoted to refining narrowly linguistic skills for passing messages. Some of that time and energy has to be re-directed to the broader issues.

To stop striving after the unattainable ideal of the native speaker, for example, immediately sets free energy for other activities. There have to be minimal acceptable standards—a different concept from that of an unattainable maximum which defines all performance as failure—but there should also be clearly recognised differentiation of standards, in accord with the variety and nature of the language being evaluated. Even a full and honest recognition of a difference in kind and therefore in standard required in speech and writing would make for better communication at every level from beginners to university students. To some extent this is the practice reluctantly accepted in teaching and examining the less able pupil, but for the more able 'standards are maintained'. There may be fears that differentiation in standards, any aiming at less than the ideal, must necessarily lead to a fall in standards. The fear can be allayed in two ways. First, the quality of communicative performance will improve with the prospect of evaluation in terms which are just as objective as any others, but which are more appropriate to the variety of language under scrutiny. Fortunately the undeniable problems inherent in this new kind of assessment are, in Britain at least, being faced in the course of introducing new public examinations. Little by little the unattainable is being replaced by the feasible and the requisite means of objective assessment are being developed.

The second way to allay fears for standards is to point out that the intellectual effort required in the understanding of other linguistic phenomena is at least as great as that required in following the intricacies of the grammatical rules of a particular written language. Part of the energy freed from striving after the unattainable might be directed into other aims: the understanding of human language and culture. Such aims cannot be defined in terms of performance and behaviour observable in precise ways at precise times. They have to be defined in terms of enriching and of raising to conscious inspection learners' intuitive knowledge of language and culture. The foreign language would here be a particular means to a general end, complemented by drawing on the intuitive knowledge of the mother tongue which the learner brings to the classroom and which is usually ignored or even deliberately excluded. Similarly, learners bring intuitions about the specific details of their own culture as well as the general conditions which determine their finding a role in their culture and society. Those general conditions include a sense of the exclusive nature, of the rightness and naturalness of the culture, which may lead to intolerance of others. It is only through dealing with such notions as part of the process of understanding another culture that the aims of tolerance and unprejudiced behaviour can be properly pursued, rather than by hoping for a beneficial spin-off from pure language teaching.

Changes in the emphasis on aims require changes in content and methods. It might be objected that knowledge of human language and culture acquired through comparative study as part of language learning would be too distant from pupils' interests. To ignore pupils' own perceptions of their needs, the argument might run, is to abandon ground already won. There is, however, growing evidence from publications and elsewhere that knowledge of linguistic phenomena can be acquired through concrete, interesting particulars (Hawkins, 1987; Donmall, 1985). The following chapters aim to provide some of the groundwork for a similar development in cultural studies. The two main extrinsic factors of motivation and success in communicative language teaching, i.e. relevance to needs and appropriateness to learners, might be usefully separated at this juncture. The 'relevance' of knowledge of linguistic and cultural phenomena perceived by pupils may turn out to have less impact on the strength of their motivation than the 'appropriateness' of the methods of teaching and assessment. Teaching which catches the interest and imagination of learners of whatever age, will rarely be challenged by them on grounds of 'irrelevance', at least in general education, where learners are accustomed to accept that there may at best be only indirect links between present learning and future career.

Let us consider then what changes in content might mean when presented in the form of a syllabus. First, there would be an account of the language to be learnt in the form of a descriptive analysis of the structure of the language and a specification of what the learner will acquire. Whether the analysis should start with syntactic structures or with notions and functions is a debate which must be pursued elsewhere. The specification for the learner will to some extent be dependent for its detail on the type of analysis chosen, but should nonetheless differentiate between kinds of usage and the minimum standards required of the learner.

The second part of the syllabus would be concerned with knowledge about language. It would consist of a series of statements about language and languages together with some indication of realisations of the statements in the mother tongue and the language being learnt. It is not envisaged that pupils should learn this series of statements any more than they are expected to learn the descriptive analysis of the particular language. The statements would have to be embodied in teaching materials, and should eventually be realised in learners as a capacity to perceive and explain, with the help of some theoretical concepts, linguistic phenomena in the languages they know. Thus learners will become 'aware' of language. One useful starting point for formulating such statements is to be found in Hudson (1981), and there are already a number of textbooks available which represent a first attempt to make linguistic knowledge accessible to school pupils (e.g. Newby, 1981; Aplin *et al.*, 1981).

The part of the syllabus dealing with the teaching of culture and cultural studies might be expected to follow the same pattern: a descriptive analysis of a culture associated with the language of study and a series of statements about cultural phenomena which may be exemplified in the home and foreign cultures. The theoretical ground for such a syllabus is much less well prepared, and will be taken up in more detail in later chapters. Yet there has to be some attempt to provide both a descriptive analysis of at least part of the particular culture and a series of statements about the nature of culture which make it possible to operationalise the aims of creating tolerance and understanding of other peoples. For without such guidance cultural studies in foreign language teaching cannot fulfil the educational role which it uniquely possesses, and which sustains the claim that foreign language teaching makes a substantial contribution to pupils' personal development and general education. Without such guidance cultural studies will never rise above the listing and learning of 'typical' differences, of haphazard facts about daily life in some conflict-free, leisure-laden, lower-to-middle class family, supplemented by a simplistic geography and history of the country in question. The present justly low status of 'background studies' in Britain will only be improved when pupils can be expected to acquire both a cognitive grasp of the patterns of culture realised in the life of (some) speakers of the language and an imaginative understanding of what it might mean to live within those patterns. This has then to be supplemented, through structured comparative study of the home and foreign culture, with a raising to consciousness of pupils' intuitive knowledge of the patterns of their mother culture. In this way a springboard to tolerance may be constructed. Tolerance of other cultures will grow more readily if pupils experience, however briefly and fragmentarily, their own culture as 'strange' and 'other', as not necessarily 'the norm'. Such a 'decentring' from one's own culture requires more than enthusiasm for another; it cannot happen merely incidentally. It must be the deliberate strategy of the teacher to bring the pupil to this kind of experience. This in turn requires that there be full recognition of this teaching as an explicit part of the subject, contributing to a widely accepted implicit aim; and such teaching needs the energy, time and resources of both teacher and pupil.

Changes in content lead to changes in method. 'Communicative methodology' will doubtless progress from its well-founded contemporary basis, taking account of developments in theories of language acquisition in the classroom context. It must also continue to take account of recent successes in stimulating motivation. To this must be added a second and a third didactic with which many language teachers will be less familiar.

The teaching of language awareness might borrow its didactic from the natural sciences, and could indeed be the product of co-operation between language and science teachers. There must be opportunity for collection of data, for observation and experiment, and the scientific mode would create the necessary distance between the observer and the phenomenon observed, which is a part of himself. The teaching of human biology may be a useful model in that it creates a distance between pupils and an aspect of their self. It would probably be much more difficult in the case of the less tangible phenomenon of language, which has an additional dimension of interpersonal behaviour in almost all its manifestations. It is through a combination of methods of language teaching in its familiar form and such a scientific didactic that the pupil might acquire 'bilingual vision', through the exploitation by the teacher of the pupil's direct experience of communicating in another language, and the awareness of language which comes from scientific observation and discussion.

The third didactic is that required in teaching cultural studies. Although questions of method and technique are discussed in pedagogical literature (see Chapter 4 for a review), much practice is based on enthusiasm and intuition, frequently accompanied by contrastive techniques, which emphasise differences between foreign and native culture. The result is a reinforcing or even a creating of the outsider's view of the culture in which the phenomena used to create and maintain group—in this case national —boundaries and group identity (Barth, 1969) are allowed to outweigh the insider's experience of the whole range of phenomena and values of the culture. The phenomena which serve to distinguish one group from another, and which are emphasised and noticed by insiders and outsiders alike are only a selection from the complex whole which is the group's way of life. To move from noticing the boundary markers to appreciating the whole complexity of the way of life is a major shift of viewpoint and experience. The outsider begins to become an insider. Furthermore, if learners are to be moved to a position where they can view their own culture dispassionately, then they must be moved, however partially, outside it by moving into the foreign culture. They must not be brought to and left at a point where a superficial outsider's familiarity with another culture might simply reinforce their ethnocentric view of what is 'natural' and 'normal'. The purpose must be to introduce them, in an inevitably partial way, to the insider's experience of the 'strange' culture as a natural and normal world. Present methods tend to stop short, leaving the learner with a recognition of boundary phenomena, a perhaps necessary but certainly only initial stage in a series of approximations ever nearer to the insider's experience. The methods need to be refined and enriched with techniques which will allow learners to use their imagination as a means to apprehending the other's position. Such methods might be adapted from English teaching, from the humanities subjects, which contribute to learners' gradual socialisation in their mother culture and which hence may indicate how a second socialisation in the foreign culture might be undertaken. To the question of methodology must be added the issue of selection: of area of experience, of the type of experience considered to be representative, of the experience likely to attract and be accessible to different types and ages of learners.

The question of change in methods and didactic focuses attention most critically on teachers and their readiness for change. Suggestions for adopting new methods to make available to learners new kinds of knowledge raise the problem of the preparation of teachers for their work, and the consequent professional identity which they gradually acquire. It is here that objections as to the feasibility of change have to be met. On the one hand, taking British experience, circumstances have already forced change onto language teachers. They find themselves teaching 'background studies' either as a part or as the whole of their activity with certain pupils. The fact that they have done so out of expediency and under the pressure of events is one reason why the result is usually unsatisfactory. On the other hand, however, they have not seen this as the kernel of their work and hence of their professional identity. This is another reason why results are unsatisfactory, and an indication that genuine change will be difficult to achieve. Yet, although the education and training which are responsible for this professional identity are unlikely to change quickly, the passage of time and experience already modify teachers' professional identity in present circumstances, for example making of the French teacher also a French Studies teacher or a teacher of Language Awareness. There is then a distinct possibility of modifying the effect of initial education and training through further, in-service education and training.

Conclusion

The argument put forward here can be summarised as follows. There is and has always been in foreign language teaching a contribution to the personal education of learners in terms both of individuals learning about themselves and of social beings learning about others. This element is profoundly linguistic because as individuals and as social beings learners are linguistic animals. It is equally fundamentally 'cultural', because language is inseparable from 'culture'. Thus as learners learn *about* language they learn *about* culture and as they learn to use a new language they learn to communicate with other individuals from a new culture. As part of this 'personal education' element of language teaching, learners are taught to *use* a foreign language. The use is primarily a question of making possible social contact with people from a different culture. However, this ability to use the language is extremely difficult to acquire in the circumstances normally existing in schools, and consequently language teachers have been much preoccupied with methods of teaching language skills, a preoccupation which has obscured and confused the issue of general, personal education. The confusion has arisen because of the need to encourage learners to persevere in the task of learning to use the language. Encouragement has been formulated in terms of tangible aims, vocational or utilitarian profits ultimately to be gained from the ability to use the language. These tangible, motivating aims have then tended to cast into the shadows other educational aims of language teaching.

Once this confusion has been recognised and eradicated, it can be seen that there are three interwoven strands in foreign language teaching; language use, awareness of the nature of language, and understanding of foreign and native culture. Each of these is integral to the contribution of language teaching to learners' general education (and consequently to their preparation for life on leaving school), and each is interdependent with the others. For example, learners' awareness of the nature of language is heightened by the experience of using a foreign language, just as understanding of foreign and native culture facilitates efficient and sensitive use of the foreign language.

However, the problems which have arisen in the history of language teaching out of the difficulty of teaching language use have led to lack of interest in methods of teaching the other two strands and integrating all three in a coherent approach to the whole of language teaching. These are problems which are in a sense internal to the language teaching profession, but which are evident to learners and therefore to other teachers, to all those professionally involved in education and indeed to the whole of society. Language teachers themselves have failed to keep a perspective on their methodological problems which would have allowed them to clarify the confusion and obscuration of fundamental educational aims.

The solution sought here and in following chapters is not in the continuing pursuit of methods for teaching language use, but in the clarification of the cultural learning strand and its relationship to the other two. The purpose is to emphasise the significance of that strand, to explain how essential it is in the contribution to general personal education and to pursue methods, materials, psychologies pertinent to it, and to the pursuit of an integrated discipline of teaching language and culture.

Notes to Chapter 1

1. Statements of the purposes of foreign language teaching are ever more frequent. In the United States there is the report of the President's commission on foreign language teaching, *Strength through Wisdom*. In Britain there has been a series of papers leading up to a ministerial policy statement, as well as the GCSE documents, and for the Council of Europe Trim (1980) has produced a framework for language learning objectives.

2. The dominance of French as a foreign language in Britain has not changed since the nineteenth century despite much talk of 'diversification' to other languages in recent years. The same dominance will be apparent in this book, despite my personal experience of teaching German as well as French. The choice of examples from French teaching is partly because they will be familiar to more readers and partly because the empirical work reported has taken place in French lessons. I would nonetheless claim that what I have to say is valid, *mutatis mutandis*, for all foreign language teaching.

3. Research funded by the Economic and Social Research Council is being carried out (1985–1988) at the University of Durham with the title 'The effects of language teaching on young people's perceptions of other cultures', further discussed in Chapter 7.

2 Foreign Language Teaching in a Multi-ethnic Society

One of the contributions of foreign language teaching to pupils' education is to introduce learners to and help them understand 'otherness'. Whether it be in linguistic or cultural terms, learners are confronted with the language of other people, their culture, their way of thinking and dealing with the world. This has been articulated most recently by Her Majesty's Inspectorate (H.M.I., 1987: 4) but has long been a fundamental belief of language teachers. Since the introduction of 'modern' languages into the curriculum in the nineteenth century, 'other people' has meant 'foreigners' in the simplest sense of the term: people 'born in another country' (Oxford English Dictionary). Today, however, there are many situations where people born in the same country are nonetheless perceived to be ethnically foreign. 'Otherness' is a feature of any society which contains more than one ethnic group and, usually as a consequence, more than one natively spoken language.

The obvious conceptual link between multicultural education—viewed as an attempt to help young people to come to terms with otherness within the society they consider their own—and foreign language teaching which has always intended to create understanding and tolerance of others, has not been forged until very recently. Let it be said immediately that the young people who need to come to terms with otherness in their own society are not just 'the majority', but also those who are 'the minorities', born of relatively recent immigration—whether 'black' or not, whether with roots in the British Commonwealth, Eastern Europe or the Mediterranean countries, whether of pre- or post-war immigration.

The link has perhaps not been forged until recently not only because it has not been noticed, but also because 'foreign' languages have an established tradition of separate academic respectability untouched by new curricular developments. The study of languages spoken by immigrants, however, is so exotic—conducted in less familiar specialised institutes of higher education—so beyond the horizons of most learners, that it has no impact on the views of most people in secondary education, whether pupils or teachers. Furthermore, the study of other languages and people outside the national boundaries has so far been conducted in ways and for purposes which are not susceptible of being immediately turned to this new focus. The conceptual link is not mirrored at the methodological and philosophical level.

Otherness in people who are by definition 'foreign' to us is not a threat to our identity. It is indeed a means of maintaining our identity, for the latter is not made up of inherently definable characteristics. It is made up of contrasts with those whom we consider different from us (Barth, 1969). Otherness within our national geographical boundaries on the other hand requires a re-definition of national identity which can be painful and may therefore be ignored for as long as possible. At another level, the techniques and methods of foreign language learning have been developed on the assumption that the foreign language is spoken in distant parts. In general all exposure to the language has to take place within the classroom; all authentic use of the language has to be imported in the form of written, audio or visual recordings, or at best in the form of a specially imported native speaker—the language assistant.

Where the foreign language is English, however, its status as an international language does mean greater exposure through the news and entertainment media, particularly in small countries such as Denmark and the Netherlands. Yet whatever the language, the learners are taken only infrequently, at the expense of effort and money, to visit the foreign country and experience the foreign language in its normal habitat. The learning of a language spoken within the national boundaries, by people who live in the same street, or indeed are sitting in the same classroom, requires modification of the foreign language teacher's assumptions and methods, and foreign language teachers are not trained in methods appropriate to second language teaching—i.e. where the language to be learned is easily available to the learners outside the classroom. Foreign language teaching is not second language teaching, methodologically speaking, irrespective of whether the educational purposes of both are similar. However, as was also pointed out in Chapter 1, language teachers have been so concerned with methodological problems that they have tended to lose sight of educational purposes and thus the nature of the link between foreign language teaching and the teaching of 'community' languages and cultures has not been discussed.

That has been the position, too, among those who are charged with keeping an inspectorial eye on or making educational policy for language teaching. As recently as 1977 in Britain, Her Majesty's Inspectorate's account of 'the contribution of modern language studies to the curriculum' spoke only of 'the people and culture of another country', of meeting foreigners at home or travelling abroad. In national terms, there is mention only of 'the development of international relationships' and of 'understanding of the unfamiliar', but without any reference to the unfamiliar which exists within national boundaries (H.M.I., 1977: 68). By 1981, however, the Ministers in charge of education in England and Wales began to ask questions about modern languages provision, one of which was formulated as follows (D.E.S., 1981: 16):

> Far more pupils than in the past now have a first language which is not English or Welsh. This constitutes a valuable resource, for them and for the nation. How should mother tongue teaching for such pupils be accommodated within modern language provision so that this resource does not wither away and the pupils may retain contacts with their own communities?

This rhetorical question is yet to be answered by the Ministers. In a further consultative document (D.E.S., 1984: 1) they have suggested that all varieties of language learning—including 'mother tongue learning'—should 'not be kept separate from each other or from modern language learning in the minds of pupils, nor in the policies of schools and local education authorities'. However, this negative formulation remains without significance as does the Inspectorate's more recent statement on the curriculum where it is claimed that 'the fact that many children from ethnic minority groups speak two languages, English at school and another language at home, can help create a context of reality for work in foreign languages' (H.M.I., 1985: 23). What 'context of reality' might mean remains unclear. The most recent draft policy statement by the Ministers leaves the whole issue still open, saying that it was too complex to deal with in the present statement and that a further consultative document would be published later (D.E.S., 1986: 4).

The most decisive policy recommendation has in fact come, not from those concerned primarily with foreign language teaching, but from the committee concerned with the whole education of children from ethnic minorities, the committee chaired by Lord Swann (*Education for All*, 1985). Having rejected the introduction of bilingual education as a means of maintaining 'ethnic minority community languages', the Swann Report states quite firmly that mother tongue provision should take place within the foreign language area of the curriculum. The report claims that there is an 'artificial distinction which has been drawn in secondary schools between what are generally termed modern or foreign languages and ethnic minority community languages'. It suggests that the pre-eminence of French and German should be challenged in 'today's interdependent world and within our own multilingual environment' and that two kinds of learner can be identified:

> Within the context of 'Education for All', we believe it is entirely right for a white English speaking pupil to study an ethnic minority community language as a valid and integral part of his education. For a bilingual pupil, we believe it is only reasonable to expect that he should be able to study for a qualification in a language in which he has some facility.
> (*Education for All*, 1985: 409)

This view, based on what is 'right' and 'reasonable', nonetheless begs a large number of questions, from the issues of methodology, through those of languages' status in the linguistic market place, to those arising from teaching both kinds of pupil in the same classroom and with the same educational purposes in mind. The report fails to recognise the crucial distinction between foreign and second languages for the 'white English speaking pupil' and the distinction between mother tongue and second or foreign language teaching for the 'bilingual pupil [who] ... has some facility'. To argue that 'facility, or even a qualification, in a community language should be seen as providing any young person with a skill of direct relevance to work in areas of ethnic minority settlement in fields such as social services, nursing and education' is to turn too quickly to fashionable terms such as skill and relevance, and to talk too easily of the applications before considering some more fundamental issues of purpose and role for minority languages.

The Swann Report is not an official policy document but the report of a committee appointed by the Minister responsible for education, the Secretary of State for Education and Science. In presenting the report to parliament the Secretary of State said:

> The Government is firmly committed to the principle that all children, irrespective of race, colour or ethnic origin, should have a good education which develops their abilities and aptitudes to the full and brings about a true sense of belonging to Britain. The Committee's report explores in detail how this principle may be made good, marshalling in the process a mass of evidence.
> (*Education for All*, 1985: Foreword)

In the British education system this is the nearest thing to a formal policy statement on curriculum as yet available, and the Swann Report thus represents the current policy approach in a highly decentralised system. Discussion of the whole of foreign language teaching in the British context has currently to take this as the base-line.

In order to clarify what the nature of this policy is, it is helpful to look at international comparisons. Churchill (1986) has described policy-making for linguistic and cultural minorities in OECD countries and analysed the underlying patterns of policy response. He suggests there is a gradation of increasingly sophisticated responses, as the complexity of the relationship between language, other sociocultural factors and the nature of education provision is recognised. In Stage 1, 'Learning deficit', learning problems associated with minority languages are said to be comparable with those created by mental retardation or similar learning handicaps. Having a different mother tongue is a 'deficiency'. This deficit approach becomes more refined in the following three stages identified by Churchill, as links with social status, affective consequences and cultural differences are recognised. Essentially the policy response is nonetheless the same: to provide instruction in the majority language, perhaps accompanied by 'multicultural' programmes to sensitise majority language speakers to the culture of the minority and to provide minority language speakers with some formal education in their own culture. In Stage 4, minority language instruction is also provided for a limited period, as a subject in the school curriculum—and occasionally as a medium of instruction—because the loss of the language may be a cause of learning problems, for cognitive or affective reasons. The purpose is, however, still to treat individuals as deficient and to make up the deficiency by whatever means, including minority language instruction, are deemed necessary.

There is a sharp distinction between these kinds of policy response and those in Churchill's Stages 5 and 6. The essential difference is the recognition of the right of the minority and the minority language to long-term survival; moreover the weaker position of minority members in education is recognised and support for the minority group provided. In this case the minority language is used as a medium of instruction, particularly in the early years of schooling, and the majority language introduced in late primary education. Only in Stage 6 is the minority language assumed to have equal rights in all spheres of public life, with extra support provided for the minority language where appropriate. Stages 5 and 6 have been attained in the Western world only by politically powerful groups sometimes prepared to use violence in their struggle: in Britain the Welsh, in

Finland Swedish speakers, in Italy the Germans, and so on. Churchill calls these 'established' minorities.

The Swann Report and the Secretary of State's statement are quite firmly within the continuum of the first four stages. For, although the Swann Report speaks in favour of maintenance of minority languages, it sees this as 'best achieved within the ethnic minority communities themselves rather than within mainstream schools' (*Education for All*, 1985: 406), supported by teaching the languages as subjects in secondary schools. Secondly, the report equates the language needs of minority language speakers with those of all pupils whose learning is at risk because of other kinds of linguistic problems: 'In many respects, ethnic minority children's language needs serve to highlight the need for positive action to be taken to enhance the quality of the language education provided for all pupils' (*Education for All*, 1985: 385). Although there is no explicit use of the terminology of deficit, the assumptions identified by Churchill are clear enough. The 'language outlook', as Churchill puts it, for the minority language as a consequence of deficit policies is for the language to be lost, with minority speakers transferring their allegiance to the majority language as soon as possible and at the most within one or two generations.

There is a further complicating factor. The implication of the Swann Report recommendations is that a deficit transitional approach can be used within the education system whilst a maintenance policy is carried out by each minority in some form of supplementary primary schooling crowned with a qualification obtained in the foreign language department in a secondary school. This combination of transition with maintenance policy does not fit neatly into Churchill's scheme and is unique among OECD countries. It is a policy which is nonetheless essentially transitional because it leads to replacement of minority language by the majority language.

What the Swann Report fails to do is to give adequate consideration to the role language plays in ethnic identity. The committee says they are

> 'for' mother tongue in the value which we attach to fostering the linguistic, religious and cultural identities of ethnic minority communities. By like token we applaud the way in which schools in our three National Regions—Scotland, Wales and Northern Ireland—have helped preserve a national identity within a United Kingdom.
> (*Education for All*, 1985: 406)

Yet they dismiss the possible linguistic comparison with Wales at an earlier point in their argument and say that the provision of Welsh through bilingual education in Wales is irrelevant to new minorities. Despite this statement the example of Wales demonstrates precisely how much an ethnic group does require a linguistic identity to fulfil and mark its ethnic identity. As Churchill points out, it is widely recognised that minority languages need more support than majority languages within the education system if they are to survive. To give them less support is equivalent to encouraging their demise, and thereby undermining one of the most important dimensions of ethnic identity. In so far as the Swann Report offers little general support for 'ethnic identity' (put in quotation marks by the report), this attitude to language is not surprising. For although the report acknowledges the significance of ethnic identity, it implies that this has to be subordinated to 'corporate identity', a concept which the report appears to recognise as its own invention by putting it in quotation marks. On the one hand the report says: 'Membership of a particular ethnic group is ... one of the most important aspects of an individual's identity—in how he or she perceives him or herself and in how he or she is perceived by others.' On the other hand it goes on to play down the importance of ethnic identity to the self and to shift emphasis to the other: 'It would nevertheless be ... naive in our opinion to deny the crucial role which ethnicity, *perhaps particularly in the "eye of the beholder"*, can play in determining an individual's place in society' (emphasis added). And having made that shift, the next stage is to emphasise the importance of 'corporate identity' over all others:

> Whilst individuals may belong to different groups of various kinds they are in addition also part of the wider national society by virtue of a range of common shared characteristics, such as a common language and a common political and legal system, which, taken together, give that society a degree of unity and its members a form of 'corporate membership'.
> (*Education for All*, 1985: 3–4)

It is thus evident that language is to be used to unify the nation and minority languages and ethnic identities are a threat to national unity, not to be encouraged and supported by the education system.

However, this implicitly assimilationist policy will not necessarily succeed in eliminating languages and identities in the time span suggested by Churchill, i.e. one or two generations. As Edwards (1977: 262) points out, language no longer used for communicative purposes on a daily basis in a minority can survive much longer through symbolic usage, often connected with religious institutions. Furthermore, Haarmann argues that though language is a basic criterion of ethnicity it is not decisive: there are settings (e.g. some Jewish communities) where the identity is marked by religious and other cultural patterns and values and where the ethnic minority has assimilated linguistically to the majority (Haarmann, 1986: 261). The strength and diversity of religious beliefs among many British minorities may well be sufficient to sustain their ethnic identity without linguistic support—or at best with the language used only symbolically and maintained symbolically in supplementary schools.

However, whatever the future may hold, it is evident that minority languages have a particular relationship to ethnic identity in a way not adequately recognised by the Swann Report. It is not surprising, therefore, that the only kind of formal curriculum recognition of minority languages suggested by the report is to equate them inappropriately and without discrimination with foreign languages. Indeed, as quoted above, the report suggests that any distinction is 'artificial', that white English-speaking pupils should study a minority language on the same basis as a foreign language, that a bilingual pupil should acquire a qualification in his/her language on the same basis and that the ultimate justification for all this should be 'providing any young person with a skill of direct relevance to work in areas of ethnic minority settlement in fields such as social services, nursing and education'. Thus the Swann Report wants to assimilate minority languages to the instrumental, utilitarian view of foreign language teaching. It in fact recommends what is already taking place in some schools, where Urdu, for example, is offered as the second foreign language as an alternative to a European language. In practice this means using second language techniques, using the lessons to discuss cultural and especially religious issues, and giving pupils the opportunity to capitalise on their existing competence in a Pakistani language to gain in a shorter course a higher qualification than they might have acquired in a second European language.[1] This is a richer educational experience than that suggested by the Swann Report.

The objections to Swann's position can be summarised as follows. The instrumental, skill-oriented view of minority languages completely distorts the meaning of the language for a member of the minority; it is divorced from the issue of identity. Second, the instrumental view of foreign language teaching in general is narrow and, as a sole justification, indefensible; it does not take account of the educational purposes of the teaching of languages spoken outside the national frontiers. Third, the meanings and purposes of minority languages for their speakers and of foreign languages for monolingual British pupils are quite different. Therefore, to place the two kinds of pupil in the same language learning setting creates problems because of the clash of purposes, even if the minority language could serve the same purpose as a foreign language for the monolingual pupil. As a consequence there would be a clash of methods too and Tosi (1986) argues that to transfer foreign language teaching methods to minority language teaching for bilingual pupils is quite misguided.

The question which now arises is whether a minority language could in fact have the same position and purpose as a foreign language in the curriculum of monolingual pupils, assuming that the clash just mentioned is overcome. If not, the second question would be what other and new role there might be for the minority language teaching for monolingual English speakers and how that might relate both to foreign language teaching and to minority language teaching for bilingual pupils.

The choice of which minority language should be offered to English monolinguals would be determined by the social context. The reason for choosing a minority language rather than a foreign language is based on the argument that by so doing there will be greater recognition of the role of minority languages within the national identity. It would therefore be unreasonable to choose a minority language spoken elsewhere in Britain but not in the vicinity of the school, for this would defeat the purpose of bringing pupils into closer contact with their own linguistic environment. To teach modern Greek in the North West of England would be to teach a foreign not a minority language, even though there are Greek communities in London.

Let us now consider our first question. In linguistic terms, a local minority language can serve the same educational purposes as a foreign language. The experience of speaking a different language, of experiencing familiar concepts in a different language and thereby gaining some new linguistic insight is in principle the same. The realisation that language is arbitrary, that others speak different languages and not simply different codes of English may even be more profound when the language differences are greater between English and non-European minority languages than those between English and closely related languages such as French and German. Similarly, where the experience of what appear to be familiar concepts is made more strange by cultural differences, the minority language would be at least as appropriate as a foreign language. It is through the realisation that the foreign language does not embody an exactly identical concept, that the concept has to be understood within a web of cultural meanings, that learners begin to gain linguistic and cultural insight.

If, therefore, the minority language were taught in the context of the culture of origin, with reference to the country of emigration—for example, Greece or Pakistan—then the function would be comparable to that of introducing pupils to a different European culture. Moreover, the more exotic, in English eyes, the culture and country, the more effective the learning might be, in terms of creating linguistic and cultural contrast from which to relativise the learner's own language and culture. On the other hand it may be that a too 'distant' culture creates insurmountable barriers for pupils in secondary schools, particularly given the practical difficulties of bringing them into direct contact with geographically distant countries. Furthermore, this approach would also be contrary to the main argument for replacing foreign by minority languages, i.e. to create greater understanding of minority cultures in learners' immediate experience. For the culture—and increasingly also the language—of the country of origin is not the same as that of the minority living in Britain. The culture imported by a generation of immigrants gradually adapts and is modified by their experience of the new culture. As a new generation is born they acquire a cultural identity which is a consequence of modification and a language which reflects and articulates the immigrant minority culture. The minority language and culture differ from those of the country of origin, which can be properly described as 'foreign'. They also differ in kind from other foreign languages and cultures.

The nature of that difference is rooted in the modifications which have to be made as a culture becomes a minority culture. Barth's analysis is worth quoting at length (1969: 31–2):

> Many minority situations have a trace of ... active rejection by the host population. But the general feature of all minority situations lies in the organization of activities and interaction. In the total social system, all sectors of activity are organized by statuses open to members of the majority group, while the status system of the minority has only relevance to relations within the minority and only to some sectors of activity, and does not provide a basis for action in other sectors, equally valued in the minority culture. There is thus a disparity between values and organizational facilities: prized goals are outside the field organized by the minority's culture and categories. Though such systems contain several ethnic groups, interaction between members of the different groups of this kind does not spring from the complementarity of ethnic identities; it takes place entirely within the framework of the dominant majority group's statuses and institutions, where identity as a minority member gives no basis for action, though it may in varying degrees represent a disability in assuming the operative statuses ...

> But in a different way, one may say that in such a poly-ethnic system, the contrastive cultural characteristics of the component

groups are located in the non-articulating sectors of life. For the minority, those sectors constitute a 'backstage' where the characteristics that are stigmatic in terms of the dominant majority culture can covertly be made the objects of transaction.

Minority languages are thus part of 'backstage' cultures, except in those rare cases where they are given equal status with majority languages, as described by Churchill's Stage 6. Given that British minority languages are unlikely to attain equal status, it follows that to teach a minority language and culture is different from teaching a foreign majority language and culture. It is in a sense a 'reduced' culture, and the language is similarly 'reduced' because it does not articulate all the sectors of societal activity as does a foreign language in its own society. Thus it would not be possible to expose learners to a complete and identifiably separate societal culture in the way that this is possible by taking them to a foreign country. This is not to say that introducing them to those backstage sectors which are articulated in a minority language is not worthwhile, but rather that it is different in nature.

Furthermore, this conceptual difference is easier to make practically visible and comprehensible to learners because of the geographical separation of a foreign culture from learners' own. For, although conceptually and in practice, the boundaries which separate minority from majority sectors are real enough, they are not always apparent to those involved and not easily visible to learners. It is, for example, easier to give pupils recognisable experience of French culture by taking them to France than it is to expose them to minority culture. For even though the geographical distance is much greater, the fact that minority culture is 'backstage' makes it less accessible to majority learners. Nandy (1981: 199) makes a similar point in arguing for the anthropological study of other societies in schools instead of current social sciences courses:

> The material used in such (social science) courses—material drawn from the children's own society—is too emotionally charged to be examined with detachment, too complex to exhibit patterns readily, too familiar to ask fundamental questions about.

There is, however, a weakness in Barth's analysis in the impression he gives that minorities cannot acquire statuses and justifications valued by all members of a society irrespective of majority or minority membership. Churchill points out that 'established' minorities can do so, particularly where legal support is given. In practice, immigrant minorities may also establish their own institutions. When a minority does break through to be 'frontstage', to establish parallel statuses and institutions to those of the majority, then the situation begins to be comparable with that of a majority foreign language. However, without legal support and public recognition, the standing of minority cultures and languages remains low. Indeed the whole argument for or against teaching minority languages to English monolinguals has at some point to encompass the issue of public attitudes to low-status languages, an issue which the Swann Report ignores and which has here been put in abeyance whilst clarifying the nature of the relationship between 'minority' and 'foreign' language and culture. That issue has now to be met in the discussion of what other purposes there might be in minority language teaching, since they cannot replace foreign languages.

There is in fact an answer to this question already existing in the practice of a number of schools. Under the label 'Language Awareness' a growing number of secondary schools—usually led by their foreign language teachers—are introducing pupils to the nature of language and languages. The purpose of Language Awareness courses is to make pupils conscious of the role of language in their lives and in the life of their and other societies (Donmall, 1985). In those schools with bilingual pupils the notion of Language Awareness is realised through introducing all the pupils' languages into the teaching (Marland, 1986: 131). The intention is to make English monolinguals aware of their multilingual environment and give recognition and status to bilingual pupils' languages in the majority institution. The Swann Report noted this development and suggests that it should be encouraged, thus giving schools a second task alongside the teaching of minority languages in the foreign language department:

> We would wish to see pupils in all schools acquiring a common grounding in the 'nature' of language, its various forms and structure, and the ways in which different language forms have been developed for different purposes, together with some knowledge of the linguistic landscape of Britain today.
> (*Education for All*, 1985: 422)

The report goes on to suggest, however, that this should be carried out in secondary schools by broadening the existing English curriculum and encouraging other subject teachers 'to be more aware of the role of language in learning'. This is a misunderstanding of the intentions of those developing Language Awareness teaching, and again assimilates the issue to a deficit model of minority languages.

The 'Language Awareness' answer is, however, almost by definition limited to language and to recognition of the importance of minority languages rather than active learning of them. It does not introduce minority culture as a course in learning the language would do. In this respect then, it goes only part of the way down the path of comprehension of the role of language in culture and identity. Were majority pupils to learn the local minority language, the situation would be different. By learning the language they would begin to experience the concepts of a different culture, as in foreign language learning, but it would be a culture which influences and contributes to the individual identity of their bilingual friends and neighbours. They would thereby be obliged to notice the 'backstage' culture and to begin to experience it in its own language in a way which is fundamentally different from simply being told about it in a 'multicultural' lesson.

The learning of a minority language would therefore differ from foreign language learning by virtue of the different relationship of the minority culture to the learners' own culture. The minority culture is not of a different 'people', in the sense of 'nation', but of a different sub-group of the same 'people' to which learners belong by national identity. Although national identity is strongly reinforced by contemporary forces in state-wide institutions, it must be remembered that the nation-state is a modern concept in Europe and the West which has gained its dominant position in determining group identity through the suppression of regional, linguistic and other ethnic characteristics. The resurgence of these repressed ethnic identities among indigenous groups evident throughout Europe (Esman, 1977; Gras & Gras, 1982; Allardt, 1979) is also evident in Britain (Welsh and Gaelic revivals) but even more striking in other countries. One of the consequences for the individual is the development of 'multiple identities' (Allardt, 1979: 39):

> Modern man does not only have multiple group membership and multiple identities, but individuals are also permitted by most social groups to be members of other associations ... It seems reasonable to assert that patterns of multiple identities will stimulate the maintenance of ethnic loyalties on one hand, but also weaken conflicts on the other.

This is more an idealisation of possible developments than a description of actual states of affairs in industrialised societies. Allardt (1979: 40) goes on to point out that it would be simplistic to assert that this would occur under all circumstances: 'If a cultural division of labour prevails together with a system of multiple identities the minority group is likely to be repressed and alienated.'

The significance of Allardt's argument for the present discussion is that it indicates that the notion of one *national* identity can give way in an acceptable and peaceful manner to the notion of multiple identities.

Indigenous, established minorities are demonstrating this and opening up the possibility for new, immigrant minorities too. Against this background, minority language learning by members of the majority will create propitious attitudes for acceptance of multiple identities at an individual level. At a state level this would mean acceptance of 'hyphenated' national identity, for example Greek-British or West Indian-British. Allardt's argument, however, also reminds us that there are powerful economic forces at work which can undermine any attempts through education to create awareness and acceptance, and in the late 1980s his warning that cultural division of labour can repress and alienate is only too significant throughout industrialised Europe.

Note to Chapter 2

1. I am grateful to Mrs Hussein and her pupils of Ian Ramsay School, Stockton for allowing me to observe lessons and talk with them about their language learning.

3 Cultural Studies within Foreign Language Teaching

In Chapter 1, three interwoven strands were identified in the web of language teaching: experience of language used for communication, awareness of the nature of language and the study of cultures. It is the purpose of this chapter to tease out the warp and weft and to investigate in greater detail the relationship between the three strands. The nature of the relationship will be significant for cultural studies in a number of ways. Above all, it will have bearing on the learning and teaching process and consequently on the constantly resurgent issue of methods and techniques. There are also such issues as the relationships between foreign and native culture both with respect to psychological development in learners and in connection with the presentation of the foreign culture. These points will be approached through the examination of the place of cultural studies within foreign language teaching, and, secondly, through discussion of the disciplines on which foreign language teaching as a whole and cultural studies in particular might rely.

The three strands identified within language teaching can be placed into two categories: language use and language awareness on the one hand and cultural studies on the other. This categorisation implies a separation of language from culture in a way which is common within the language teaching profession and which seems to have a commonsense and intuitive basis, at least where pedagogy is concerned. The extracting of language from the cultural whole in order to concentrate the learners' minds on it is a standard practice within language teaching, although various 'bilingual' approaches—for example in Canada (Swain & Lapkin, 1982)—teach language by leaving it embedded in other cultural phenomena for much of the time. The question arises whether this pedagogic separation for methodological reasons has any other justification or in fact corresponds to the nature of the phenomena. The relationship between language and culture, whether in general or in a particular case, is of course an extremely complex problem which has psychological, sociological and political dimensions, each worthy of study beyond the confines of this book. It would, however, be shirking responsibility to proceed to discussion of the learning of language and culture within language teaching simply on intuitive or commonsense grounds. The following is no more than an attempt to discuss the relationship in general with the particular purposes of language teaching in mind.

A number of distinctions can be made. First there is the fact that language, and language variety—dialect or sociolect— is one of the overt signs of cultural identity which people meet daily in their lives. Individuals use language varieties with varying degrees of self-awareness to signal their social identity, often 'accommodating' their language to the requirements of situations and interlocutors (Giles & Powesland, 1975). This factor is relevant to the question of whether the study of French, for example, should lead to interest in a wider area than metropolitan France. In so far as there are Belgian, Swiss, Algerian, etc. varieties of French, each nation or region is linguistically independent and might therefore be studied independently of the others. On the other hand, because of the tradition of modelling these varieties on metropolitan, Parisian French—seen as the ideal, pure form—there is a link with *la Francophonie* as a whole which transcends national boundaries and might be considered a reason for widening the scope of interest beyond the frontiers of France. The same point might be made in a different way. It is only the traditional dominance of France which makes us start with France and perhaps move outwards. Why not teach the French of Belgium or Quebec? Within France, too, regional varieties and dialects are signs of regional culture; the significance of the Langue d'Oc in a meridional culture is only one, well-known example. All this points to the fact that, for individuals or for whole groups, regions or nations, language is a way of marking cultural identity comparable to other cultural markers such as dress, housing, or social institutions.

Language differs, on the other hand, from other cultural phenomena in that it is used to refer to other phenomena and has usually to be used to refer beyond itself. To wear a particular article of clothing is to make a choice within the system of clothing and to make a statement about clothing which also has connotations of personal, social and perhaps political attitudes. It is also possible to express social and political allegiance through choice of language variety. Speaking a social class dialect is an expression of allegiance in so far as the speaker chooses to keep his dialect or switch to another. Using the vocabulary of communism is a means of signalling political convictions. But language is always about something else; one cannot speak the dialect, use the vocabulary, without referring to something else. Often, in fact, the language is transparent, inconspicuous. In a working class milieu a working class dialect is not a conspicuous choice by the speaker. In a communist milieu the term 'alienation' is accepted currency in debate. The emphasis in both cases is on the meanings and message the speaker is immediately concerned to express. Yet in a middle class milieu, the working class accent deviates from the normal and inevitably connotes certain values and is interpreted as a statement of social allegiance. In a non-communist milieu, the use of 'alienation' requires explanation and that explanation involves raising to critical awareness the normally accepted meanings of words. In negotiating meanings, we agree on normal denotations. For example, there is a contemporary process of re-negotiating the meaning of 'work' in a society without employment for all. From meaning 'labour' carried out for money used for buying food and clothing and so on it is in the process of being redefined as 'activity to develop social interaction and occupy leisure time'. It is in the course of this process that some fundamental values of our society are clarified and made available for inspection.

Thus language pre-eminently embodies the values and meanings of a culture, refers to cultural artefacts and signals people's cultural identity. Because of its symbolic and transparent nature language can stand alone and represent the rest of a culture's phenomena—most successfully in the literary use of language—and yet it points beyond itself and thereby constantly undermines its own independence. Language in use by particular speakers is constantly referring beyond itself irrespective of the intentions of the speaker: language cannot be used without carrying meaning and referring beyond itself, even in the most sterile environment of the foreign language class. The meanings of a particular language point to the culture of a particular social grouping, and the analysis of those meanings—their comprehension by learners and other speakers—involves the analysis and comprehension of that culture.

The pedagogic separation of language from culture is thus justified in the sense that language can and does stand alone. It does so most obviously in literature, and the long association of language and literature teaching is some explanation for the separation. On the other hand, the tendency to treat language quite independently of the culture to which it constantly refers cannot be justified; it disregards the nature of language. That tendency is not necessarily an intended distortion of language and is seldom taken to its potential extreme. No doubt all language teaching contains some explicit reference to the cultural whole from which the particular language is taken. Even where a deliberate attempt to transfer its use to a different culture is made, as in those countries where English is taught from textbooks which refer only to the native culture of the learners, the absolute separation of lexical items from their original reference is extremely difficult. There is, however, a need to take more careful account of the implications of separating language from culture for pedagogic reasons, particularly when, in the foreign language context, the representations of that cultural whole are largely limited to the foreign language classroom, and learners' experience of the foreign culture is largely vicarious. Thus although the warp of language can be teased out from the weft of culture, the learner needs to see the web of the whole, and this has methodological implications.

There is considerable discussion in the literature of the significance of the fact that a foreign language (FL) learner is a native speaker of one or more languages (e.g. Klein, 1986). Questions of 'interference' or transfer are predominantly focused on syntax and phonology. As soon as semantic interference or transfer arises, however, the interdependence of language learning and culture learning begin to become evident. For the association of an L1 meaning with an FL word is a cultural transfer; the FL word is being used to refer to an L1 cultural phenomenon. In other words, just as teachers expect to cope with syntactic or phonological transfer/interference, they must also beware of cultural transfer/interference and cope with it appropriately. The detailed discussion of what such coping does and might mean will be left for later. The argument thus far can be summarised in the deceptively banal statement that language learning is culture learning and consequently that language teaching is culture teaching. We move now to the question of the disciplines to which language and culture teachers may look for support in this situation.

Language teaching depends, for help and guidance in the teaching of syntax and phonology, on linguistics and, in the increasing concern with functions of language, on pragmatics and sociolinguistics. That is, in so far as language teachers attempt to give learners more than grammatical competence, taking note of Hymes' (1972) and others' definitions of 'communicative competence', language teachers find themselves relying on analysis of how native speakers use the particular language for social intercourse. Such sociolinguistic analyses introduce culture-specific pragmatic uses of language and begin to uncover some of the values and norms of the culture for the language teacher (Riley, 1984). Sociolinguistics is therefore a necessary and natural extension of the linguistic disciplines to which language teachers must look.

However, in addition to the cultural meanings carried by the functions of language, language it has been argued above embodies the values and artefacts of a culture through referential meaning. In order to teach these linguistic meanings, the language teacher has need of an analysis of the values and artefacts to which they refer, an analysis which is other than linguistic. For the language teacher needs a discipline on which to depend for this aspect of his teaching just as much as linguistics is the discipline underlying the teaching of syntax, pragmatics and phonology, or awareness of the nature of language. The academic discipline which has concerned itself with the analysis of other cultures—as a step towards understanding the fundamental nature of man—is social anthropology. The techniques of cultural analysis developed in social anthropological investigation of cultures radically different from the native culture can also be applied to give accounts of cultures more familiar to us, including our native culture. The effect is to make the familiar strange and therefore more accessible to conscious awareness and inspection. Ethnomethodologists (Douglas, 1970) have used these techniques as a means of academic analysis of aspects of Western societies. This may prove a useful avenue for the language and culture teacher to explore as a source of accounts of target cultures, as an authority on the nature of particular cultures and the notion of culture in general.

Of course, in practice there is no single authoritative view within anthropology of what is meant by 'culture'. The view adopted here—and justified in more detail in a later chapter—is the 'symbols-and-meanings' conception of culture, associated with Geertz and others. It is a rejection of the behaviourist-influenced view of culture as individuals' environmentally influenced capacities to adapt appropriately to existence in a particular society. Geertz's formulation defines culture as 'an historically transmitted pattern of meanings embodied in symbols, a system of inherited conceptions expressed in symbolic form by means of which men communicate, perpetuate and develop their knowledge about and attitudes towards life' (1975: 89). Such a view clearly puts language, as one of the principal carriers of meanings, at the centre of an account of a particular culture, and reinforces the argument made above that language teaching inevitably involves teaching culture. In this view, to teach culture is to teach the systems of meanings and the symbols which carry the meanings, symbols both linguistic and non-linguistic.

Before taking further this question of teaching content it may be profitable to take another perspective: the specification of curricular aims. Thus far we have examined the relationship of the phenomena 'language' and 'culture' as they exist in the world. The curriculum development perspective allows us to consider how those phenomena can be studied in secondary education.

The determination of curricular aims has been dominated in recent years by the notion of behavioural objectives. Stenhouse has provided a general critique of this model, summarised in the statement: *'Education as induction into knowledge is successful to the extent that it makes the behavioural outcomes of the students unpredictable'* (1975: 82, emphasised in original). Whereas skill in language use *may* be susceptible to training and measurement in behavioural objective terms, an issue which I do not propose to treat here (cf. Byram, 1979), knowledge about language as a human characteristic and knowledge and experience of another culture have an educative purpose in individuals' personal development, for which behavioural objectives cannot account. Only with a behaviourist view of culture is it conceivable to specify learning aims in terms of behavioural objectives, but a symbols-and-meanings view is more open-ended. In this view individuals acquire a competence to interpret social phenomena and to determine their own behaviour in ways which are consonant with the meaning systems shared by all the members of a society. To teach foreign culture in this sense is to introduce pupils to new meaning systems and their associated symbols, to provide them with the opportunity to acquire new competences and to allow them to reflect upon their own culture and cultural competence. What effect this might have on individuals is impossible to predict, as Stenhouse argues for all induction to knowledge.

The alternative to the use of behavioural objectives put forward by Stenhouse—the process model of curriculum design—requires the adoption of the 'principles of procedure' from a field of knowledge or discipline, and the disciplines of linguistics and social anthropology would appear to be the source of such principles for the two components of language teaching which are based on bodies of knowledge rather than skill-training, i.e. language awareness and cultural studies.

Although Stenhouse expresses the view that the objectives model is inappropriate for 'induction into knowledge', he does not discuss initiation into social norms and values—or systems of meaning, as we called them above—at any length, except to say that the deliberate promotion of norms of behaviour could be expressed in terms of behavioural objectives. Yet where there is *education* in values, the objectives model is inappropriate. For it implies an engineering of pupil behaviour which is at odds with the nature of knowledge and values. Therefore Stenhouse proposes the alternative of determining content and methods from within the disciplines or forms of knowledge. The advantage of his proposal is that content and methods are not a reflection of pre-determined objectives, nor do they themselves determine any particular set of outcomes. This is the potential role for social anthropology in cultural studies: the traditions of enquiry and analysis as well as the established body of knowledge in the academic discipline would be the basis from which appropriate teaching would be developed at secondary school level.

There are, however, some problems. First of all, social anthropology, though more than one hundred years old, is still a discipline which is evolving its basic procedures. Second, the objects of study—exotic and relatively simple and self-contained societies—are of a different nature from the societies associated with foreign languages usually taught in British and other Western schools. Furthermore, social anthropology is precisely at a stage when it is partially withdrawing from study of exotic 'simple' societies and seeking to extend its methods and applications to the kind of societies which are the interest of language teachers. Now, although this promises to be very convenient for language teachers, it is perhaps not the best time to look to social anthropology for guidance (Jenkins, 1985). Finally, social anthropology is not one of the 'central' disciplines which are easily associated with the school curriculum in the way that natural sciences, history or even literary criticism are.

On the other hand, there is some previous experience of drawing on anthropology for the school curriculum, in the example of 'Man: a Course of Study' (MaCoS, 1968–70), and this may offer a very valuable starting point for developing content and methods in cultural studies. There are two aspects of 'Man: a Course of Study' which should be emphasised immediately. First, it shows how the complex and powerful issues of an academic discipline can be presented to 10- to 12-year-old pupils. What could be more 'abstract' and 'difficult' than the content of the course as described by Bruner (1966: 74)?

> The content of the course is man: his nature as a species, the forces that shaped and continue to shape his humanity. Three questions recur throughout. What is human about human beings? How did they get that way? How can they be made more so?

A course of cultural studies, oriented towards francophone culture, especially France, might be formulated in a not dissimilar way:

> The content of the course is man in his particular manifestation in French culture: the particularity of French culture as a dimension of the humanity of people born and raised in it. Three questions are fundamental: in what ways does the cultural dimension of their nature make people French and not British, or French and not Japanese, for example? How can people who are, in a similar way, uniquely British understand French culture and communicate with French people? How

might this experience of French people and culture affect British people?

'Man: a Course of Study' realises its abstract content through a number of concrete studies, and it is the invitation to speculate on the nature of man through these concrete studies which is important. There is no attempt to provide an exhaustive coverage of the topic or even an introduction to the practice of social anthropology. The complexity of French culture is also such that some kind of selection must be made. In current practice notions such as 'relevance'—to the postulated needs and current interests of the pupil—or 'typicality' are used on an intuitive basis. If the emphasis is as much on speculation as on comprehensive and/or representative coverage of 'the topic', then some of the problems in selection are less pressing.

The second point to be emphasised is Bruner's recognition of the problem of teacher expertise (1966: 74):

The first and most obvious problem is how to construct curricula that can be taught by ordinary teachers to ordinary students and at the same time reflect clearly the basis or underlying principles of various fields of inquiry.

The solution proposed is that teachers become learners alongside their pupils, but superior in certain learning skills and, more important, in their understanding of the rationale of the process in which they are all engaged. On the one hand this would be reassuring to language teachers with no training in the human/social sciences, with nothing more than their personal and perhaps partial experience of the foreign culture. On the other hand, it is in the nature of most language teaching until recently that the teacher is the dominant if not the sole provider of knowledge, and the role of learner is one which language teachers more than some others would find difficult to accept. There would, moreover, still be requirements on them to understand the rationale of the course and this implies familiarity with and interest in a social science perspective. There would still be a need for careful preparation as the MaCoS experience, with its specially created training courses, demonstrated.

A third point brings us back to methodology and teaching content. 'Man: a Course of Study' is based on a wide range of materials among which film is vital. The practicality of video-playback in secondary schools makes the inclusion of film in cultural studies feasible as well as highly desirable. In addition, the language teacher has the opportunity of taking his pupils to the country in question, which 'MaCoS' teachers do not have—it is much less easy to organise a trip to study the Inuit of Canada. Thus it should be clear that 'people study' (Lambert, 1974) is accessible in principle to all kinds of pupil. This would mean, however, a redefinition of foreign language as a practical, science-based subject with appropriate financial support.

Lambert's (1974) proposal is a radical 'Alternative to the Foreign Language Teaching Profession' in which he suggests that the lack of interest among American pupils for language learning could be remedied by making the language process 'incidental not only to the communication process and the learning of content taught via the language, but also that it be made incidental to the learning about different peoples and their styles of life' (1974: 60). His proposal may be too radical to be acceptable to a profession which identifies as *language* teachers, and his further suggestion that the focus should be on 'the cultural mosaic at home' (1974: 58) within the United States borders—now comparable to the situation in European countries—ignores the significant differences created by territoriality (Bochner, 1982). Lambert's argument is, however, also founded on his wide experience of bilingual education in North America which points to the success of language teaching for 'practical communication' being dependent on the language being used as a medium rather than an object of study. Dodson (1967) too has discussed language teaching techniques as a result of his experience of bilingual schools in Wales. He also identifies two levels of attention to language but suggests that both levels should be part of the methodology, that teachers need to exercise pupils' command of the forms of language, as well as to have a subject which they teach through the language. Hawkins (1981) suggests that Dodson's two levels can be further defined into four, with differing degrees of concentration on the content and on the learner's involvement in it. There is, moreover, some experience of using a foreign language as a medium of instruction in the *'sections bilingues'* of secondary schools in Britain and in France. For example, in one school the two levels, language as an object of study and language as medium, are clearly separated in the organisation of the teaching. French is taught as a subject for two years and then pupils are also introduced in the second year to the separately timetabled subjects *'géographie'* and *'l'homme et son environnement'* which are taught through the medium of French (Hadley, 1983). Although such programmes are limited to a very few schools, the length of experience gained is quite considerable and could well prove useful to the teaching of cultural studies, as will be argued in a later chapter.

In theoretical work developed under the label 'Communicative Language Teaching' and in experimental work in India, reported in Brumfit

(1984), the arguments have developed in a similar direction. Communicative competence, it is argued, can be best created by task-oriented study, by problem-solving methods which are pupil-centred. In this concentration on task and problem and pupil-centred learning, foreign language teaching is in step with other educational change; there is a happy convergence of language learning theory and general educational theory. There is, however, one particular dimension of language teaching which still lacks thorough discussion: the nature of the task or problem. In bilingual education, the content taught in the second or foreign language is taken from the normal school curriculum, ranging from mathematics to history. In the problem-solving experimental approach in India the problems appear to be specially designed for the language lesson to be conceptual, culture-free tasks, and in communicative language teaching in mainstream education pupils are given 'information-gap' tasks (Littlewood, 1981) which are either culture-free conceptual tasks or which simulate transactions between tourist and native as they might take place in the foreign language society. Thus in bilingual education the choice of content is determined by factors external to the aims of language teaching, and in foreign language teaching the tasks are chosen mainly according to the degree of conceptual difficulty or linguistic complexity or the frequency of the transaction in tourist encounters in the foreign society. The criteria for the choice of problem or activity do not include consideration of the incidental messages which pupils may be receiving. The emphasis on problems and transactions may leave pupils with the perhaps undesirable impression that foreign language learning is an apprenticeship in confrontation relationships with people from another country, where the problem is to obtain certain consumer goods or services.

Lambert's (1974) suggestion implies quite different criteria for the selection of content, although he does not expand this point himself. If the object of study is a people and their culture, then the criteria are surely to be found in social anthropology, the discipline devoted to the study of people and culture. Social anthropology needs to be the basis of the definition of precisely what the content might be from which a selection is made. In other words, the description of the potential content for a study of 'French people and culture' should be carried out on social anthropological grounds. The selection from the potential content—which is clearly too vast to be included in its entirety—must also be carried out on criteria developed partly in social anthropology and partly in pedagogy and psychology. For the selection from the numerous and complex phenomena contained in the phrase 'French people and culture' must be non-arbitrary, must be made on grounds of what is in some sense central to the culture, influenced by considerations of pedagogical feasibility and of the psychological development of the pupils.

For if learners are to understand aspects of the foreign culture in the traditions of social anthropology, i.e. as participant observers, then the aim must be to participate in it and experience it from within, as well as observe it and understand it from without. Any other perspective would be insignificant because it would leave learners firmly planted in their own culture, judging the foreign culture by inappropriate standards, seeing the foreign culture from a tourist viewpoint and failing to apprehend the nature of the intimate relationship between the language they are learning and the culture it embodies. Furthermore, part of the contribution to learners' personal education from language learning is to offer them a perspective on their own language and culture, a viewpoint from which to perceive their own experience and selves as social beings, to relativise and contextualise their own culture by experience of another. This question of perspective is bound up with the issue of cultural analysis.

Consider the experience and knowledge which learners bring to the classroom. Hundeide (1985) argues that we base our interpretation of people's actions on a 'repertoire of recurrent episodes and routines from everyday life ... a shared collective structure organised as episodes that reflects the regularity of life within a society with a particular social structure, culture, language, history and ecology'. Others have described this kind of repertoire in terms of schemata (Rumelhart, 1980; Schank & Abelson, 1977) discussed in more detail in Chapter 6. This repertoire is taken for granted, is a tacit background of expectancies which are not normally accessible to the individual. It is only when the unexpected occurs and has to be interpreted that we become aware of our normal expectancies. The deviations from the norm may be of two kinds. Firstly, the 'level of intensity' of a phenomenon may change and be noticed. Secondly, there may be a deviation from a category or dimension of experience, i.e. a new kind of experience which by contrast makes us aware of the limitations of our experience hitherto. Midgley (1980: 305–6), citing Lorenz, suggests that social norms and rites develop in human groups much as species and sub-species develop phylogenetically their peculiar characteristics and properties. The resulting divergence erects barriers between groups and has been termed 'pseudo-speciation':

> ... it can work only if whatever the culture dictates is taken for granted most of the time as unthinkingly as noncultural activities would be among animals. Constant hesitation and arguments would make adaptations ineffective. Accordingly, people everywhere are inclined, until they meet different customs, to assume that their own are universal, and when they do meet them, to suppose that they are not dealing with members of their own species at all but with some sort of

inferior imitation which it is probably all right to massacre. Pseudo-speciation interferes with the 'sentiment of humanity' and can lead to intolerance and violence.

Benedict (1961: 5) makes much the same point in a cross-cultural perspective:

So modern man, differentiating into Chosen People and dangerous aliens, groups within his own civilisation genetically and culturally related to one another as any tribes in the Australian bush are among themselves, has the justification of a vast historical continuity behind his attitude. The Pygmies have made the same claims. We are not likely to clear ourselves easily of so fundamental a human trait, but we can at least learn to recognise its history and its hydramanifestations.

Originally written in the 1930s, the last sentence is particularly resonant. Midgley and Benedict warn of dire consequences of cultural egocentricity, and the assumption that one's own customs are universal or, more insidiously, natural. For if people consider their own cultural behaviour is 'natural', i.e. condoned by some spirit or force which is intrinsically 'great and good', it is a short step to assuming that all other behaviour is unnatural and therefore to be disapproved and even destroyed. Ochs & Schieffelin (1984: 284) draw attention to the role of anthropology in this respect with reference to fundamental issues in Western countries:

comparative material can lead us to reinterpret behaviors as cultural that we have assumed to be natural. From the anthropological perspective, every society will have its own cultural constructs of what is natural and what is not ... The issue of what is native and what is nurtured (cultural) extends to patterns of caregiving and child development. Every society has (implicitly or explicitly) given notions concerning the capacities and temperament of children at different points in their development and the expectations and responses of caregivers are directly related to these notions.

If foreign language teaching contributes to re-interpretation of pupils' own behaviour by introducing them to those in other cultures, it can surely claim to have a significant role in young people's education.

Let us consider the particular case of English pupils learning French and being presented with an account of how French people live, in the course of their language learning. Typically this account will be largely incidental to the process of language learning, and be evident in accompanying pictures, in the narrative texts used for language teaching, in information sections separate from the language study. The account will therefore include deliberately chosen and accidental elements and will typically emphasise those which are different from comparable elements in the learners' native culture. If we consider pupils' perceptions of this account, the implication of the preceding quotations is that they will tend to focus, with or without the help of textbook writer and teacher, on those elements which are 'unnatural', i.e. different from their own customs, behaviours and systems of meaning. In Hundeide's terminology they will focus on deviations from English normative expectancies. Yet the phenomena they notice may not deviate at all from French normative expectancies or, if they do, they deviate in level of intensity rather than category or dimension. Inevitably then the attitude engendered towards those phenomena is that they are deviant, odd, strange or abnormal. This is more likely to reinforce 'pseudo-speciation', as Midgley puts it, with the accompanying tendency to despise rather than accept French culture and civilisation.

To summarise the argument so far in this chapter: we have dealt with the relationship between language and culture and the necessity to teach both in an integrated way, and with the introduction of social anthropology as a parent discipline to language and culture teaching, alongside linguistics and in particular sociolinguistics. The integration proposed is influenced by bilingual education programmes where the language is both object and medium of instruction. In foreign language teaching, the language needs to be taught as an object of study, but also used as a medium for teaching and learning. The proposal is that it should be used as a medium, not for problem-solving, but for teaching and learning about the people and culture associated with it. There is some experience of using the foreign language as a medium in 'sections bilingues', where the object of study is the human geography of the country and its people. The present proposal is to introduce a different academic discipline, and the methods associated with it. This discipline, it has been argued, is most suited to fulfilling the educational aims of raising understanding of and reducing prejudice towards other cultures and peoples. It also provides the academic foundation and security for an approach to curriculum development which is focused on a well-formulated process of teaching and learning rather than the pre-determination of behaviourally defined learning outcomes. Here too there is some experience to be drawn on, in Bruner's work, although adaptation would be required for foreign language teaching.

The claim that language teaching improves intercultural relationships is therefore potentially justifiable if changes are made in the teaching of culture as an integral part of the subject. However, as has already been briefly indicated, it is also necessary to take account of pupils' existing cultural knowledge and experience if the potential for attitude and perception change is to be realised. This requires consideration of how pupils' interpretation of a foreign culture is influenced both by their established expectancies or schemata and by the selection of experience made for them by textbook writers and teachers. This is an area which demands separate treatment (Chapters 5 and 6) but it is useful at this point to exemplify the issues by reference to some work in social psychology and social anthropology.

Let us start with the kind of perspective represented by Hundeide. According to this view, a cultural phenomenon will come within the scope of consciousness if it deviates from a standard of normative expectancies. The norms are set entirely within the culture and help the individual to interpret experience in that culture. Yet, although individuals do not take up a standpoint outside their culture, they are nonetheless aware of the existence of other cultures and of the fact that other individuals perceive them in turn 'from outside'. In reacting to the outsider and the outsider's presumed viewpoint, individuals may become conscious of different phenomena from those which would otherwise push themselves into their awareness. It is in coming face to face with the outsider that individuals need to establish a group or social identity which they support through identifying distinctive and critical features of their cultures which serve to separate them from the outsiders. Social identity is part of an individual's self-concept, according to Tajfel, deriving 'from his knowledge of his membership in a social group (or groups) together with the value and emotional significance attached to that membership' (quoted in Gudykunst, 1986: 4). If the group membership at a given moment is created *vis-à-vis* an outsider from another country, then it is the individual's ethnic identity which comes into focus, that part of his social identity which arises from his knowledge of belonging to a particular ethnic group.

Barth (1969: 27) lists four aspects of the term 'ethnic group', designating a population which: (1) is biologically self-perpetuating; (2) shares fundamental cultural values, realised in overt unity in cultural forms; (3) makes up a field of communication and interaction; (4) has a membership which identifies itself, and is identified by others, as constituting a category distinguishable from other categories of the same order.

He argues that the fourth is the critical feature for identifying an ethnic group, since overt institutional forms may be determined by ecology and transmitted culture; diversity in overt forms need not signify ethnic diversity. In this light, the Frenchman of the sixteenth *arrondissement* in Paris is as French as the peasant farmer in Auvergne through self-ascription and ascription by others, despite the wide diversity of their cultural experience and institutions. However, the basis of self-ascription—the aspects of behaviour which the insider identifies as characteristic—may differ from the basis of ascription by others. Furthermore the features which are identified in self-presentation by insider to outsider may differ from self-presentation to insider, adapting to the stereotype which the insider believes the outsider to hold of him.

A further dimension in the complexity is the possibility, following Barth, of there being socially stratified groups with their own sub-cultures. Thus although the peasant from Auvergne will identify with the Parisian in some ways and in certain situations, he will equally emphasise the differences in other situations. The group he identifies with may be regional, occupational, national or ethnic depending on the dichotomies which are in operation at any given time.

There emerges from this a need to identify a level of grouping (ethnic, national, regional) at which to begin analysis and presentation of the culture to language learners. Second, it is necessary to be aware that the features which are most apparent at a given level are a function of the dichotomies present at that level and are not necessarily an exhaustive account of the characteristics of the culture of that level. Third, the features a member of the group may present are potentially influenced both by the insider's self-presentation to insiders and by his beliefs about the stereotypes held of him at that level by outsiders.

In order to exemplify the argument consider the following questions which might be asked with respect to the culture associated with teaching the French language:

At what level should analysis be made? *La Francophonie mondiale? La Francophonie européenne? La France metropolitaine? La France régionale?* or, in a different set of categories which partly overlap with the first: *la bourgeoisie? la classe ouvrière? le citadin? le campagnard? le Parisien? le méridional?*

In what terms should the analysis be made? Societal institutions? Cultural artefacts? 'Overt signals or signs—to show identity ... dress, language, house-form, or general life-style ...' (Barth, 1969: 13). Value orientations in interaction with insiders or outsiders ('basic value orientations: the standards of morality and excellence by which performance is judged' (Barth, 1969: 14))? Or in terms of the symbols-and-meanings conception (Geertz, 1975) to which institutions, artefacts, signs and signals would be considered subordinate, simply realisations of the patterns and meanings of culture?

Contemporary answers to the questions of level of analysis are to portray the culture of a lower middle class, city-dwelling (often Parisian), ethnically metropolitan (usually north of the Massif Central), non-extended family with traditional sex and familial roles. Yet the contemporary learner population in Britain includes pupils from all social classes, from nuclear, extended, one-parent, matriarchal, role-changed families, with Anglo-Saxon, Indian, West Indian, Welsh, Scottish and many other ethnic origins and allegiances (and concomitantly with a variety of mother tongues); a similar situation can be found in other European countries. In order to respond to this variety, on the assumption that learners' interest and sympathy will be best aroused by material portraying people on some dimensions comparable to themselves, we need to consider portraying a much wider range of people.

Questions about terms of analysis are most often answered implicitly; some 'auxiliary' material addresses itself explicitly to societal institutions (school, transport, sport) or to cultural artefacts (art, literature, dress, housing). Both 'auxiliary' and textbook material portrays implicitly social, familial roles, and habitual routines and customs. All these are limited to the particular sector of society described above. There are also two other kinds of limitations in contemporary material. First, it does not portray —except through literature and non-literary extracts at an advanced level—Barth's 'basic value orientations' of even a limited sector of society. It is usually only at an advanced level and through literary study, in particular at higher education level, that there is any attempt to study the systems of meaning of French society and their symbolic realisation in cultural artefacts. There is, however, a clear connection to be made here as Geertz implies when referring to the analysis of culture: 'Analysis, then, is sorting out the structures of signification—. . . the enterprise [is] like that of a literary critic—and determining their social ground and import' (1975: 9).

Second, there is no attempt—except at an advanced level—to move from description to interpretation and explanation. These two criticisms are linked in that explanation would involve reference to the values and meanings which underlie the institutions, artefacts and routines portrayed. This is not to say that the choice of what is to be portrayed is arbitrary. It is determined partly from a need to arouse pupils' interest through things which are comparable, partly from the desire to make pupils aware of differences, partly with an eye to material connected with the language being learnt at a given point, partly with a view to the needs of a visitor to

France and the motivation that this offers. The position is nonetheless unsatisfactory when interpretation and explanation is left to a stage when only a tiny percentage of students are still engaged in language learning.

In considering how improvements might be made, we need to bear in mind both the wider scope required by a heterogeneous learner population in contemporary language teaching, and the argument that perception and understanding require shifts in viewpoint. Taking the latter point first, our earlier analysis indicated that cultural phenomena are experienced against a background of normative expectancies. If simple assimilation to the learner's own culture is to be avoided the phenomena must be framed in the expectancies of the target culture. Simple similarity and difference across cultures is not a sufficient basis for selection and analysis. 'Normative expectancies' are, however, not part of the consciousness of the individual and the analysis required must go beyond simply portraying the 'overt signals or signs' to which Barth refers. An explanatory level of analysis is required, both as a basis for selection of phenomena and in the presentation of phenomena, since it is in explaining the values and expectancies of the target culture that the learners' viewpoint can be shifted towards that culture away from their own. Widening the scope of the analysis, for example, to a greater variety of social and ethnic groups in France, in turn requires refinement of the analysis of values. For, assuming that each group has a sub-culture, it is necessary to analyse the values and meanings of each sub-culture as part of the presentation of phenomena from it and to emphasise its particular traits.

Consider the following example. Many people in France have a second home, often a house in the country. Treated simply in cross-cultural comparison, this phenomenon could be described with the help of statistics, showing how much more common it is in France than England, how it is not restricted to the upper middle class, how the taxation system makes this possible for a wider range of people. If we consider the values and beliefs of the upper middle classes, the *'maison de campagne'* is an extension of their living space, a factor enhancing their standard of living. For many of them, the choice of region is made on grounds of convenience, attractiveness and price. Their connection, if any, with the region through family origins in particular, is a minor factor. For working class families the factors are reversed in importance. Connections with an area, the intention of returning to the area are the significant factors, leading to a willingness to accept a lower standard of living in their first home in order to maintain a second home. In both cases, however, there is a common trait. French life is marked by the overbearing centralism of Parisian domination, in cultural, legal and governmental senses. Yet the provinces and in particular the countryside are considered to be a source of strength for city-dwellers, especially Parisians. Therefore, for all classes, the *'maison de campagne'* is the means of overcoming the town–country, Paris–provinces dichotomy. In this analysis then, what deviates from English expectancies is the idea that working class people have second homes and, the English assumption is, a standard of living equivalent to that of English upper middle classes. This seems odd and even self-contradictory. In the context of French values, however, the self-contradiction disappears and it is the common ground of overcoming the town–country dichotomy which is the normal expectancy. The aspects which distinguish the French from the English—the significance of family origins and 'return'—are the ones which would become conscious to the English because they deviate from the English norm. For the learner, then, there would be the contrast of two 'internal' viewpoints, and the 'drawn-back' viewpoint which allows him to perceive the difference between English and French attitudes to the town–country, metropol-province dichotomy.

Conclusion

The argument that cultural studies is an integral part of language teaching, because of the relationship of language and culture, has led to the notion of a disciplined study of a culture. The study and acquisition of language—language in use and language awareness—must take place in the context of cultural study and the discipline which shall provide the procedures for cultural study is social anthropology. The complexity of the journey to be travelled from academic study of exotic peoples to the secondary school foreign languages classroom is not underestimated. Anthropologists have given only infrequent attention to the study of Western European cultures, and then mainly in their traditional forms of village life (for a study of France see Wylie, 1966). Yet, because in their studies of exotic groups they have isolated fundamental common phenomena, it might be expected that conversely in the study of super-ficially similar cultures anthropology will clarify the differences. Leach (1982: 18) puts it as follows:

> The differences between the primitive societies which anthropologists like to discuss and [the] modern industrial societies ... belong to the level of macro-economics and macro-sociology. At the level of dom-estic and inter-personal relations with which most people are concerned for most of each working day, the superficial contrasts are simply different transformations of a single complex of ideas about the proper relationship between men and things and men and other men.

Leach here stresses the notion of underlying common concern and simultaneously points to contrasting ways of dealing with common experience. From the point of view of foreign language teaching, both are important. The traditional claim that language learning and foreign travel creates greater tolerance of otherness is no doubt based on the notion of all human experience having, at some fundamental level, common ground. On the other hand what Leach calls 'superficial contrasts' can create resistance and prejudice even with first-hand experience, unless learners understand that they are precisely 'superficial'. And though superficial, these contrasts are crucial to language learning for without proper realisation of their significance, transfer and interference from native culture will obscure the relationship between the foreign language and the cultural context. Study of the culture thus has two purposes which are interdependent: to facilitate learners' use of language and to help learners apprehend the concept of cultural 'otherness', what Leach calls the 'constant puzzle in all kinds of anthropological enquiry', that is, 'the problem of how far we are all the same and how far we are different'.

4 Contemporary Views on Cultural Studies

Research and scholarly discussion of what I have called the third strand in the web of language teaching has in some countries' traditions been a recognisable characteristic of work on language teaching, and elsewhere has been no more than perfunctory. In no sense can it be said to have been afforded universally the serious consideration it deserves, but this is scarcely surprising when one considers the ways in which methodological issues of instilling skills in language have dominated the history of modern foreign languages. Nonetheless, there is a worthwhile literature, particularly in the German tradition of *Landeskunde*, within which the present essays need to be placed.

The question of terminology can be dealt with initially and with relative ease. The best established term is that used in Germany, '*Landeskunde*', meaning literally 'knowledge of the country'. The French term '*civilisation*' refers in a broad sense to the way of life and institutions of a particular country. In the United States there is a tendency to use the word 'culture' to refer to learning about customs and behaviours associated with language learning, thus concentrating largely on daily life. In Britain, the phrase used in secondary schools is usually 'background studies', referring to any knowledge which supplements language learning, largely concentrated on information about customs and daily life with some reference to social institutions. In higher education the term 'area studies' has been created to distinguish courses which are not devoted exclusively to literature, as used to be the dominant tradition. The term 'cultural studies' used throughout this work is not used in British education, or indeed elsewhere, although it is not entirely new (cf. Kramer, 1976, for example).

The following review follows roughly some of the issues dealt with in preceding and subsequent chapters. It will be noticed, however, that some questions, such as the position of cultural studies and foreign languages in multicultural education, are not treated separately because there is little or no work to review. Another area which does not require separate treatment for the same reason is empirical research. On the other hand, it would have been possible to trace separately the origins and development of the German *Landeskunde* tradition, as its history has been carefully documented. In practice, although the review has been divided into several sections, these are mainly to provide some degree of clarity and there are a number of overlapping issues and contributions appearing in more than one section.

Cultural Studies in General Education

As was pointed out in earlier chapters, the place of cultural studies in the school curriculum is dependent on the overall justification for foreign language teaching in general education. This dependency relationship is usually unquestioned and is likely to remain so in most education systems. Kacowsky (1973) surveys aims of language teaching and cultural studies in a number of countries and summarises statements from UNESCO and the Council of Europe on the importance of teachers being trained in cultural studies. In general he found that the dependency relationship was a common factor; the survey needs to be up-dated to be entirely reliable. That there need not be such a relationship is apparent in situations where foreign language teaching has a different role from that assigned to it as a result of its growing out of the tradition of teaching classical languages discussed in Chapter 1. The special nature of English as the dominant language of international communication as a result of large-scale colonisation, past and present, can lead to reassessment of the relationship. Arguing that foreign language teaching aims to instil new values in the learner, values associated with the language and culture, Alptekin & Alptekin (1984) suggest that teaching English as a Foreign Language in Third World countries can lead to cultural colonisation, because the culture of the English-speaking world is implicitly contrasted with that of the learner's own, to the detriment of the latter. They suggest that the model which the learner is required to pursue should be explicitly that of the successful bilingual rather than of the monolingual and monocultural native speaker of English. In this way, the learner can be helped to operate in two cultures without devaluing either. On the other hand, Lambert (1974) suggests as a consequence of his work on bilingual immersion programmes, that learners should have their attention focused entirely on 'people study'. Pupils would learn about other people and, by using the foreign language to do so, would learn the language incidentally. This is the principle which has been applied to a limited extent in some '*sections bilingues*' of secondary schools as already noted in Chapter 3 and will be further developed in Chapter 8 (King, 1975; Hadley, 1983).

It is evident then that the common assumption that language learning leads to learning about the native speakers of a language in order to understand, accept, tolerate or even assimilate to their values and way of life may not be appropriate in all situations. However, where the assumption is appropriate, a number of views of the dependency relationship are tenable.

Reviewing '*Landeskunde*' in Germany, Buttjes (1982) identifies three basic positions on *Landeskunde*. The first, 'pragmatic-communicative orientated', means teaching about the culture which is intended to alleviate problems of communication in the language when the learner visits the foreign country (cf. Kruger, 1981). This leads to a tourist's view of the culture and a selection of materials accordingly. The second approach is to give learners a critical understanding of the foreign people, of their own view of themselves and their values. This he calls 'ideological-understanding' orientated.

The third position develops this notion of critical understanding, but encourages learners to go beyond mere acceptance of particular historical developments and present social situations as inevitable and unalterable, to respond critically, analytically and, as a consequence, to analyse their own social environment with critical understanding. The label attached to this third position is 'political-action orientated'. Grindhammer (1978), quoting Tabbert and Ziegesar, makes more sub-divisions. '*Kulturkunde*' was, in the inter-war years, a means of encouraging appreciation of German culture through contrast with English-speaking countries. A second stage was the attempt to foster democracy in German learners by immersing them in British culture. A third aim was to prevent misunderstandings among peoples and cultures. This differs from the more pragmatic fourth view—Buttjes' first category—which wants to prevent individual misunderstandings. She then challenges the dependency relationship of culture to language by claiming that 'culture learning is actually a key factor in being able to use and master a foreign linguistic system', and not just a 'rather arbitrary claim that culture learning is a part of language teaching' (1978: 64). There are two characteristics of this article which are peculiar to the German scene: the historical development of a number of purposes for cultural studies (cf. Buttjes, 1982; Kerl, 1979; Humphrey, 1978; Harnisch, 1976; Kramer, 1976) and the close connection between university and school debates on the nature of cultural studies.

In Britain, there is similar discussion of area studies in universities and polytechnics, but the link with school work has not been made. Despite numerous articles on teaching techniques, 'authentic' materials and so on, attempts to discuss the fundamental principles of the place of cultural studies in secondary school language learning are infrequent (Byram, 1983 and 1984). In France, there has been a recent revival of interest in the teaching of *civilisation* evident in collections of articles (e.g. Poirier & Rosselin, 1982). Most significantly, however, there has been a wide-ranging treatment by Zarate (1986) which develops a thorough theoretical and methodological approach while offering practical illustrations.

In comparison with both France and Britain, however, the undoubtedly greater complexity and subtlety of thinking about cultural studies in Germany is a result of a much longer history of pedagogical concern (Schrey, 1982; Raddatz, 1977). The historical burden of fascism has also been an influence. As Kramer (1976: 139) puts it, the fascist influence made cultural studies an instrument for creating a greater sense of *'Gleichschaltung'* in 1935 of modern language teaching in Nazi Germany. He suggests that since the war cultural studies have been dominated by attempts, in reaction to fascist influence, to make cultural studies value-free, usually by making them subordinate to communicative efficiency. In the English-speaking world, the issue of values has been ignored and subsumed under the purpose of producing greater understanding and tolerance, the values of which are implicitly positive. This is the position, for example, in a statement of aims for the new GCSE examinations in England, Wales and Northern Ireland. A similar position is fundamental to 'La Charte des Langues Vivantes' where, in opposition to the narrow utilitarian and mercantile conception, a view of language teaching is proposed which offers the opportunity 'd'épanouir sa personnalité, sa sensibilité, d'apprendre et de s'enrichir par la connaissance d'autre langues et la confrontation féconde avec d'autres cultures sans aucun préjugé de limitation' (1980: 310) (cf. Chapter 1 for detailed comment). In the Bellagio Declaration of the European Cultural Foundation and the International Council for Educational Development in 1981 the following view is maintained: 'for effective international co-operation, knowledge of other countries and their cultures is as important as proficiency in their languages' (van Els, 1982), and such knowledge is dependent on foreign language teaching.

The assumption that cultural studies will be an aid to efficient communication and co-operation is further reinforced by recent emphasis on 'communicative competence' as a broader concept than 'grammatical competence'. For 'communicative competence' involves an appreciation of appropriate language use which, in part at least, is culture-specific. This recent development is therefore a renewal and extension of the auxiliary, pragmatic function of cultural studies.

Uhlemann (1979) discusses at some length the influence of this relationship on the nature of cultural studies, and its aims and materials, in the German Democratic Republic. He links cultural studies with the issue of international understanding and, writing within a socialist perspective, requires that cultural studies shall contribute to the development of 'sozialistischer Persönlichkeiten' and further 'den objektiven Prozess der sozialistischen Integration und der weiteren Annäherung der sozialistischen Nationen und Völker' (1979: 233). In this case the value-laden nature of cultural studies is explicit enough. Both Kerl (1979) and Kramer (1976) point out, however, that in West Germany, the pragmatic emphasis, whether in its early post-war form or in its more recent relationship with communicative competence, has been assumed to be value-free. Their critique of this assumption is also useful in questioning and making explicit the further assumption that, though not necessarily value-free, cultural studies can only be of positive value.

Kramer (1976: 142–3) argues that the attempt to make cultural studies subordinate to communicative ability is an attempt to be neutral:

> Hierbei liegt der Akzent darauf, dass kommuniziert werden soll und nicht WAS WIE WARUM. Die Perspektive ist total pragmatisch: der Schüler als zukünftiger Konsument, Tourist oder Kontaktperson mit einem Fremden im eigenen Land.

Buttjes (1982) reiterates this point, saying that, in this perspective 'affirm-ative Bilder sollen die Kontaktbereitschaft anbahnen'. Thus the issue of critical attitudes is avoided and there is the temptation of providing a false picture of 'Merry Old England' or America as the land of opportunities (Buttjes & Kane, 1978). For Kerl (1979: 157) the weakness of this 'agnostic position' is also evident in the lack of a systematic procedure in methodology, in the emphasis on solid pieces of individual information rather than an attempt to give a view of the whole culture, in the tendency to teach cultural studies indirectly and incidentally to the teaching of language. This 'flight into pragmatism' as a means of avoiding ideological issues is, says Kerl, itself a political position and to deny this is to deceive oneself.

Furthermore, this position does cultural studies a disservice (Kerl, 1979: 158):

> Indem der gesellschaftswissenschaftliche Charakter der Landeskunde geleugnet wird, entzieht man ihr den Boden, auf dem allein sie sich entwickeln kann. Ein solches Vorgehen kann auch nicht mit dem

Hinweis auf die politische Pervertierung kulturkündlicher Zielsetzungen in der Zeit der Faschismus gerechtfertigt werden.

In the British situation, it is not the wish to react against political perversions of the past, but simply a lack of serious consideration of the issues, which has produced the present state of affairs. Yet the present state of British affairs is accurately characterised by Kerl's description of 'agnostic' methods and by Kramer's and Buttjes' references to an orientation which prepares pupils to be unquestioning tourists, 'consuming' the foreign culture, both as a means of improving communication efficiency and as a means of creating understanding between peoples. Thus the tendency in British policy documents, and in the attendant but tacit philosophy, to assume that the acquisition of 'a healthy curiosity towards foreign peoples' (H.M.I., 1977: 68) incidentally and as 'background' to language learning is unproblematic, in content and methodology, is profoundly self-deceptive.

It is probably as a result of this assumption that something worthwhile will emerge provided the language teaching is itself adequate, that there is so little concern in Britain with training teachers in cultural studies. Student teachers often claim that their own enthusiasm for and love of 'the country' will be the basis for their attempt to 'broaden pupils' horizons' and it seems that this is the assumption on which they are allowed to go forward. For there is no theoretical discussion of the place of cultural studies in teacher training beyond the debate about 'area studies' as part of teachers' first degree. In the only detailed survey of courses preparing students for modern language teaching (Spicer & Riddy, 1977) it was evident that very little time was given to the teaching of 'civilisation'. The situation may have changed in the meantime, but there is no evidence of concern with the issues in the form of academic articles.

The position in West Germany is different. The tradition that some undergraduate degrees are vocational and lead to a teaching qualification and nothing else has led to a greater concern that the content of such degrees should be directly related to the curriculum of schools. Nonetheless, a survey in the 1980s of German universities (Haas & Schrey, 1983) revealed a situation which was unsatisfactory in the view of the authors, both in respect of the teaching of cultural studies to university students and especially with reference to the number of courses dealing with the didactics of cultural studies in schools. Students were not sufficiently taught, nor adequately trained to teach cultural studies:

> Angesichts der universitären Landeskundepraxis verwundert es nicht
> mehr so sehr, dass der Landeskunde-Aspekt des schulischen Englisch-

unterrichts in den Titeln der fachdidaktischen Veranstaltungen so selten thematisiert und in Praxis meist nur nebenbei behandelt wird. (Haas & Schrey, 1983: 406)

This is not to say, however, that some writers have not given serious consideration to the question of teacher training in cultural studies. Humphrey (1978) provides a schematic survey of the position of cultural studies in West German education and then draws conclusions for teacher training in universities and proposes possible courses in some detail. Buttjes & Kane (1978) also sketch a course and offer an outline bibliography. Grindhammer (1978) describes her work at the University of Hamburg and then discusses how the demands of officially determined school curricula make it imperative that future teachers should have a thorough grasp of the culture(s) associated with the language they teach.

Before sketching their particular course Buttjes & Kane (1978) raise the question of the disciplinary basis of work in cultural studies, and Humphrey (1978) considers the ways in which cultural studies might be integrated into existing sub-divisions of university language courses. The question of where and on what basis cultural studies might be covered at university level is crucial to the question of aims. For example, if cultural studies are understood to have a critical, political, emancipatory purpose—rather than a supposedly value-free information one—then the teacher should, it may be claimed, have a training in the social sciences and not just in literary criticism, as has been the tradition. Clearly, the question of parent discipline and the training of teachers also has bearing on the methods used towards particular aims. Furthermore, the question of what is considered appropriate content for cultural studies, and in particular the issue of selection, gradation and order of presentation of content, will be influenced by the emphasis accorded to the parent discipline(s).

Kohring & Schwerdtfeger (1976) take semiotics as their starting point. Since, for them, culture is communication, semiotics as the science of communication is the natural basis. From this they propose to take two sub-disciplines for the analysis of culture/cultural studies: syntax and pragmatics. Above all, this position is intended to offer a means of cultural analysis, describing how natives of the culture communicate in the culture. Secondly, the analytical tools are applied to the various approaches to a foreign culture open to a learner, to the ways in which a learner relates to the communication system of the foreign culture on the basis of the communication system of his own culture. To varying degrees learners may attempt to assimilate the syntactic and pragmatic patterns of the target culture to those of their own and will be variously encouraged to do so by the different approaches in teaching methods (cf. Kacowsky, 1973). Or they may also to varying degrees attempt to work within the syntactic and pragmatic patterns of the foreign culture without filtering them through their own.

Dressler, Reuter & Reuter (1980) take their starting point in the concept of 'communicative competence' and suggest that since this competence involves interaction in a foreign culture, they consider that the ethnography of communication will provide a framework for the proper integration of cultural studies into language learning. The framework will identify the different aspects of speech acts which a learner must master to be competent. Some of these will be culture-specific conventions and rites, but this framework does not handle propositional knowledge about the foreign culture, and is open to criticism of illusory neutrality mentioned above.

Buttjes (1982) identifies three areas of interest within Germany. In Romance studies the emphasis is on comparative analysis of countries, using a social sciences basis (cf. also Baumgratz & Neumann, 1980). Thus specific differences are isolated against a background of comparable basic sociopolitical structures. In German studies, project work of a multi-disciplinary nature identifies particular themes treated in linguistic, literary and historical terms, without comparison between the foreign and native cultures. In English studies, there is an attempt to use social and cultural history as a basis for analysis, supplemented by the subjectivity of experience captured in oral history. These three different approaches are concerned with ways of analysing the foreign culture, rather than with teaching methods. In this latter respect Buttjes identifies two broad directions: the analysis of meanings of words and texts as means to identifying the particularities of the foreign culture, and the contrastive analysis of pupils' experience of their own and the foreign culture. Buttjes & Kane (1978) suggest that cultural studies should be considered a social science. In particular they see a need to balance empirical, systematic social sciences with hermeneutic, historical human sciences, suggesting that social anthropology offers an adequate balance between *Sozial- und Geisteswissenschaft*.

Keller (1983a and b) takes his position from social psychology. Considering cultural studies to be a means of creating greater understanding between peoples, he uses the tools of social psychology to establish the stereotypes of a foreign people and the autostereotypes held by that foreign people. One of the purposes of language teaching is to produce better matches between these two.

Kramer (1976) refers briefly to developmental psychology in his observations that the learner who finds his way into another culture by learning the language does so on the basis of a certain stage of development of linguistic socialisation. He may come to terms with new experience by means of cognitive processes of assimilation and accommodation, and foreign language learning can thus be a 'contrastive broadening' of the original process of cultural socialisation.

It is especially remarkable that all these various borrowings and dependences on a number of academic disciplines contrast with the usual training of languages teachers in the United Kingdom. Although languages may be studied together with many other disciplines (to be detailed in a survey funded by the Nuffield Foundation) either in an integrated way or, more often, simply simultaneously, the majority of teachers are trained in literary criticism and appreciation and not in any of the social sciences. This poses considerable problems.

Cultural Analysis for Pedagogical Purposes

The lack of parent disciplines has a further effect: the pedagogical grammars developed within linguistics and applied linguistics have no parallel for cultural studies. It is therefore not surprising that much effort has been expended on filling this gap.

In determining how to limit the potential object of study and then to analyse it, it is the ultimate pedagogical purpose which should be decisive. Since cultural studies is dependent on language learning some forms of analysis may be more appropriate than others. An analysis of culture as a system of communication (Hall, 1959; Guthrie & Hall, 1981; Dressler, Reuter & Reuter, 1980) is more comparable to the analysis of language itself, than is, say, the analysis of cultural artefacts in separate genres—for example, analysis of social institutions or the analysis of artefacts of craft or art.

Furthermore, the decision on the kind of analysis to be undertaken will determine the kind of analytic instruments and methods. Thus, Guthrie & Hall (1981) suggest that ethnographic methods are most appropriate. The ethnographer attempts to describe the culture from within, interpreting the significance of particular phenomena as they operate within the semantic system of a particular culture, at an emic level, but also needs some starting point, some framework with which to get the first grip on the phenomena at the etic level (i.e. drawing on the distinction between phonemic and phonetic description current in linguistics). This is the kind of general framework offered by Hall's (1959) Primary Message Systems, 'ten separate kinds of human activity . . . only the first involves language', which together make up a culture.

The anthropological bias of Hall's (1959) work is not surprising, because of the long history of association between linguistic analysis, language learning and anthropological fieldwork. Anthropologists and 'qualitative' sociologists meet the problem of learning as well as analysing another culture most forcibly in language (Deutscher, 1968). It is not surprising then that Keller (1983a) looks to anthropological models of culture as a basis for pedagogical models as does Lambert (1974). In analysing the conceptual framework of cultural studies Keller suggests that three different models of culture may be variously appropriate to different age groups of children learning a foreign language. The behaviourist model analyses culture as patterns of behaviour acquired and transmitted through symbols, and is appropriate for early stages of learning (cf. also Oksaar, 1983 and Seelye, 1974).

> Die behaviouristischen Forschungen bieten zum ersten Mal wissen-schaftenlich untermauerte Ergebnisse für typische Verhaltensmuster, die als Grundlage fur die Informationsvermittlung vor allem in der Unterstufenunterricht dienen könnten.
> (Keller, 1983a; 201)

A functionalist analysis of the interdependencies and causes of cultural developments would, on the other hand, go beyond surface phenomena and be more appropriate to the level of interest of older pupils. A Marxist model further reveals conflicts of interest and resistance to existing power structures: 'deren Behandlung im Unterricht nicht nur sachlich gerechtfertigt ist, sondern zur Steigerung der Motivation beitragen kann' (Keller, 1983a: 202). He then develops a framework model of the many factors which make up a modern social system.

Firges & Melenk (1982) look to ethnomethodology since for them the starting point of cultural studies shall be the experience of everyday life of the native of the foreign country. In ethnomethodology they seek the systematic representation of the everyday knowledge which the native possesses unconsciously, but which the non-native has to handle consciously. They further suggest that it is in language and texts that this foreign reality is to be found, and thus language and cultural studies have to be integrated. Their emphasis on everyday life also leads them to identify a number of themes—family, habitat, work and so on—which would guide the analysis.

The integration of linguistic and cultural analysis is also found in various pragmalinguistic analyses in the sociolinguistic literature. These do not have specific pedagogical purposes directly in mind, but are clearly written within the general concern to elucidate 'communicative competence'. Marquez (1979) analyses kinship terms in Tagalog and English as a means of making contrastive analyses of aspects of culture; this is like the kind of analysis known as '*Lingualandeskunde*' in the German Democratic Republic, with its roots in contrastive analysis and reminiscent of Lado's (1957) earlier attempts to identify pedagogical problems. Richards (1982) contrasts conversational strategies across cultures, and Riley (1981, 1984) and Thomas (1983) discuss culturally determined 'pragmatic failure'. Hoops (1982) sketches some of the issues of text selection and treatment from a pragmatic viewpoint. Loveday (1982) discusses the culturally specific presuppositions and expectations which language learners need to be aware of and able to handle, but points out how little is known and how lacking in methodology language teaching is in this respect. The path leading from the detail of fine pragmatic analysis of discourse exemplified in Riley and Richards, to the much larger scale of propositional knowledge about a foreign culture's major institutions and artefacts and the structure which underlie them remains uncharted. Keller (1983b) points out that a behaviourist model is unsatisfactory because it deals with surface phenomena, and suggests functional and Marxist models for older pupils. In the course of this shift, pupils will move from the 'knowing how'—pragmalinguistic, competence-orientated—to 'knowing that' which makes the learner conscious of the knowledge which the native has both consciously and unconsciously. But because Keller, with Kramer (1976), believes that cultural studies should have an emancipatory function, the knowledge that the learner acquires should also include a critical dimension, an understanding of underlying factors which goes beyond the everyday knowledge of the native. In this view, then, the emphasis of Firges & Melenk (1982) on the acquisition of native-like experience of everyday life is insufficient. On the other hand, this may well serve as the link between the micro-analysis of pragmalinguistics and behaviourism and the macro-analysis of functionalism, Marxism or the like.

One other approach to cultural analysis is through the social psychological notion of stereotypes. There are two aspects: stereotypes as a layman's means of coping with experience of other peoples, and stereotypes as a scientific concept for use in analysis. Both Hsu (1969) and Duijker & Frijda (1960) attempt to analyse complex modern societies through the notion of national character or stereotype. Both attempt to categorise the values which national groups hold and according to which they seem to behave. Gadoffre (1951) adds credence to this approach by isolating national images and the values they incarnate, and also raises the issue of how these images can be changed and re-interpreted by other groups when they cross national borders. Lambert & Klineberg (1967) undertook a major survey to examine stereotypes held by children in an attempt to establish how the stereotypes arise. Keller (1978, 1979) has undertaken investigations to establish young British people's views of their own national character (autostereotype), young German learners' views (heterostereotypes) and the effect of language learning, especially through visits to the country, in creating convergence between the two. Keller (1983b) sees this as one of the aims of language teaching thereby facilitating communication and under-standing.

Finally, Picht (1975) suggests with respect to higher education that students should be taught critical approaches arising out of a number of disciplines. Thus materials need not be 'representative' since students study cases rather than acquire factual knowledge. This is in tune with Sten-house's (1975) approach to curriculum planning for secondary education which was discussed in Chapter 3.

Learning Theory for Cultural Studies

If cultural analysis is to be influenced by pedagogical aims, both of these need to be related to the learning process. Yet there is even less work on the processes in which learners may be presumed to be involved. The literature reviewed in this section does not amount to theory, and indeed much of it does not address the main issue directly at all. That issue is whether a theory of how pupils 'learn' a foreign culture can be developed to such a point that pedagogical and didactic consequences may be derived from it. To draw on the analogy with language learning theory is an obvious first step for two principal reasons. If culture is considered to be primarily a number of communication systems (Hall, 1959), then it can be assumed that theory concerning one of the systems—language—can be helpful in describing others. The second reason is derived from pedagogical practice. Since culture is 'learnt' in the language teaching classroom, then it will be at least convenient that didactic methods for each are derived from similar sources. This may pre-determine the issue too soon, and there is work in cross-cultural psychology which must not be forgotten (Triandis & Lambert, 1980; Brislin et al., 1975; Bochner, 1982).

Those authors who attempt to develop psychological insights into cultural identity for a second or foreign language learning context deal with the identity of the individual and, secondly, with the attitude of the individual towards others. Social psychological research into attitudes towards foreign peoples is reviewed by Cooke (1973) and most recently by Gardner (1985). Cooke considers work on attitude origins and change, and suggests methods which might be incorporated into language teaching in order to change ethnocentric attitudes. Gardner reviews research on the relationships between attitude, motivation and achievement in language learning, but does not address cultural studies directly. Intuitively there would seem to be a link between attitudes and perceptions, but the research on attitudes remains for the moment tangential. The several British attitude surveys (Burstall, 1974; Schools Council, 1981; APU, 1985) tell much about attitudes to the subject 'French', but little or nothing about perceptions of 'the French'. On the other hand, in discussing stereotyping, Keller (1983b) describes five cognitive processes which are used to simplify perceptions of other peoples and suggests a number of criteria for deciding if cultural studies can render simplifications more differentiated and liable to create better conditions for understanding others' views of themselves.

A number of authors discuss cultural impediments to communication created by incommensurability between cultures. Difficulties can be overcome, Müller (1980) suggests, by learners acquiring part of another conceptual system through 'confronting' key words and concepts in one culture with those of another, thereby identifying points of contact and difference between phenomena which may be superficially similar. D'Angelan & Tucker (1973) suggest, however, that ethnic background may significantly limit the match between the foreigner's and the native speaker's connotations for a particular word. Byram (1984) discusses this question of the need for learners to take the perspective of the other culture if they are to understand it. Triandis (1975) suggests a means of modelling different kinds of difficulties of cross-cultural communication and then raises the question of 'culture-training', of making learners capable of handling the difficulties. Oksaar (1983) also suggests that learners have to learn norms of cultural behaviour as they learn language, and attempts to identify 'culturemes' of behaviour for learners to acquire. However, none of these authors suggests what psychological processes might be involved in these changes of perspective or acquisition of cultural behaviour.

Another approach to the question of learning theory may be made through consideration of children who acquire two cultures and two languages as part of their socialisation: 'natural' bilinguals. It is worth distinguishing those who learn their languages and cultures before they start formal education and those who find that on entering school they are entering a different linguistic and cultural world. For this second group have a well developed linguistic and cultural repertoire already; they are likely to have less individual attention from adults; their attitudes towards others' languages and cultures are developing simultaneously with their second language and culture acquisition and so on.

Yet despite the vast literature on bilingualism and bilingual education, there is relatively little on the psychology of biculturalism. Hamers & Blanc (1982) review the psychological literature on ethnocentricity and discuss the nature of bilingual cultural identity, in which they suggest language is a far less significant factor than in monolingual cultural identity. They discuss the relationship of monolingual cultural identity to the learning of a second or foreign language and the barriers to be overcome. This is the approach in Schumann (1978) who lists a number of psychological factors—'culture shock', social dominance, assimilation—which may inhibit successful second language learning. Stauble (1980) also discusses acculturation as instrumental in the process of acquiring a second language. She describes a number of reports which suggest that 'second language learners will succeed in learning the target language to the degree that they acculturate to the target language group', and Brown (1980: 132) describes four successive stages of acculturation. Yet we still lack an account of the processes of acculturation as part of the psychological development of the child. This issue will be taken up in more detail in Chapter 6.

Materials and Methods

The literature reviewed so far has been largely concerned with establishing the nature and role of cultural studies, attempting to build theory from which teaching materials and methods could be developed. Since cultural studies is, however, already part of language teaching, it is also important to examine practices. This may lead to changes which are intuitively sound but also to the development of theory inductively, grounded in empirical observation and analysis. It is this perspective which has led to evaluation of materials and methods.

Given the significance of textbooks in language teaching it is scarcely surprising that numerous evaluations are carried out. However, attention to the cultural studies dimension is often missing. Even in the German literature there is a dearth of work concerned directly with criteria for analysis, although the need is recognised (Buttjes & Suck, 1977). The issue can be approached in two ways: through the analysis of existing books and through the postulation of ideals for developing new books. Some authors link the two.

In order to arrive at justifiable criteria, it is necessary to be explicit about premises. Huhn (1978) begins from the point of view of the aims of cultural studies, of which he emphasises two: enhancing the understanding and co-operation between peoples and contributing to pupils' political and social emancipation. Buttjes (1982) makes the point that a view of cultural studies as an acquisition of foreign sociocultural meanings is particularly well served by working through visual and spoken media and texts as well as written ones. Krüger (1981: 26) takes the communication-orientated view that cultural studies content should be determined according to 'inwiefern sie Kommunikation fördern oder behindern und zweitens unter welchen Bedingungen sie überhaupt Kommunikation ermöglichen und für den Sprachlerner sinnvoll sind'. Coming from a quite different pedagogical tradition, Andersen & Risager (1979, 1981) see foreign language teaching as 'a factor in the socialisation of the learner' (1981: 23) and therefore require that textbooks give a true experience of the society they claim to represent. They suggest that textbooks often give the impression of ideological neutrality—in both cultural and linguistic terms—but in fact any selection of content or language variety carries ideological overtones. This point is also made by Poirier & Rosselin who point out that distortions can arise out of the target culture's own dominant view of itself (1982: 178).

Andersen & Risager's general criterion is then the concept of realism, although they do not adequately explain what is a notoriously difficult term, in literary criticism for example. For them 'the social content has to be representative in such a way that it can be regarded as a sort of summary of that society. Of course, the selection is not independent of one's own view of society, of the social theory adopted and of the categories used' (1981: 31). Keller (1983b: 155) also stresses the importance of avoiding unconnected items of information and giving instead insights into the social norms and conflicts and the underlying structures of a foreign culture. Although there are many questions still unanswered here, these authors have at least grasped the nettle of representativeness. This is not the case, for example, with Joiner who embraces the aim of promoting positive attitudes but begs all the questions when she writes that language students must be given 'an objective and accurate picture of the country whose language they are studying' (1976: 243). In addition to the assumption that there is only one country for each language, she uses the term 'objective' as if it were unproblematic, and goes on to imply that the view of the language teacher evaluating materials is the decisive one.

On the other hand, Joiner is prepared to offer specific guidelines, an evaluation form for textbooks. It is a mixture of a checklist of the number and variety of elements and of evaluation—in one place incorporating a semantic differential. It is crude, rests on unspecified values and she does not make any suggestions as to how the form results shall be analysed once they are complete. It is also possible that content analysis will be of help (André, 1983); it has been applied to the socio-economic analysis of primary school textbooks in France (Mariet, 1982).

Andersen & Risager's model for analysis is one of the most rigorous. It is derived from models for analysing realistic prose, presumably in literary criticism. They suggest (1981) four wide categories for implicit and explicit information about the foreign society:

— the spheres of activity and consciousness of the persons (subjects of conversations, norms and values)
— verbal and non-verbal interaction (nature of social relationships, sex and generation roles)
— explicit information about the country or countries (historical, geographical, contemporary, social etc.).

They also require that different, appropriate varieties of language should be exemplified for the range of social groups included.

Huhn (1978) establishes seven criteria dealing largely with the treatment of content, although he claims to be dealing with content itself.

— factual accuracy and contemporaneity of information in cultural studies—an a priori point which raises immediately the question of keeping books up to date
— the avoidance or at least relativisation of stereotypes—by making pupils conscious of them
— the presentation of a realistic picture, not one which implies the foreign society is problem-free (this is the point which Andersen & Risager have developed in detail)
— freedom from, or at least the questioning of, ideological tendencies in the material—pupils should not be encouraged to accept the dominant image of society, whether foreign or their own, but rather to question it, partly through comparison
— the comparative dimension further requires that phenomena be presented in their structural, functional contexts rather than presented as isolated facts—a view shared by Andersen & Risager, and of significance for the view taken of the appropriate model of cultural analysis (cf. Keller (1983b) discussed above)
— the sixth and seventh criteria are concerned with the presentation of historical material: its relevance to understanding contemporary

society should be explicit, and where presented through personalities it should be made clear that they are products of their
age.

Huhn also raises the question of presentation, and the potential bias arising
from fictional presentation of cultural studies content, and from editing of
authentic texts without indicating the points of excision.

Huhn draws conclusions from his criteria as to how the teacher might
correct any failings in the materials used. Andersen & Risager go on to
outline their plans for producing materials which will live up to their
criteria. Others take this general direction too. Poirier & Rosselin (1982) are
particularly concerned that material should be seen in context, both
contemporary and historical, and present two models of culture which
would help to situate any one phenomenon. As a means of explaining
contemporary phenomena historically, they suggest that Pierre Bourdieu's
Questions de Sociologie might be particularly fruitful. Buttjes (1982: 153)
follows Huhn in warning against stereotyping and personalised history. He
enumerates briefly his general criteria for a project 'English Across
Cultures':

> fremdkulturelle Binnenperspektive statt eigenkulturelle Aussenper-
> spektive, Primärquellen statt Sekundärdarstellungen, Selbstzeugnisse
> Betroffener, Vorrang nichtfiktionaler Texte vor fiktionalen, vielseitige
> Nützung der Texte, Sequenzen der Texte als Angebote zu plan-
> mässigem landeskundlichen Lernen.

In a more recent article Buttjes (1983) explores the potential of Oral History
as a source of texts for cultural studies (see also 1981 and 1982). Ziegesar
(1978) suggests that trivial literature should be used because it is here that a
people's view of itself—and he makes the connection with Keller's autostereotypes—is clearest and most accessible. Kruger (1981), who puts the
emphasis on cultural studies as an enhancement of communicative effect-
iveness, suggests that the Council of Europe's foreign languages work
should be consulted to establish which themes should be chosen and lists 15
from the work on German as a foreign language. Porcher (1982) also draws
on the Council of Europe's work on needs analysis to establish a number of
questions which must be answered in developing a well-founded approach
to teaching culture, which he suggests is far from present in language
teaching in France. Deutschmann (1982) also argues for the development of
a needs analysis, depending on the target group of learners; he distinguishes
'*handlungsbezogenes Landeskunde*' from '*informationsbezogenes Landeskunde*', a distinction which could be helpful in deciding on aims, gradation
and order of presentation. Whereas Baumgratz (1982), dealing particularly

with the teaching of French in Germany, raises the point that the specific historical and contemporary relations and mutual views of the home and foreign countries should be taken into consideration when deciding on context. Returning to Andersen & Risager (1981: 32) we find that, having grasped the nettle of representativeness, they find themselves before the didactic question of balance between a representative selection of people from the society and a confusing number of persons. They propose

> to select some families or groups living together [who] represent different social groups or strata ... in different situations, different relations and contacts with each other, and this will hopefully provide an adequate description of their total life situation.

Teaching methods are partly a function of materials, and the selection of materials will be influenced by the methods envisaged. Discussions of methods are therefore usually found with materials analysis. Less frequently, the discussion of methods is linked to psychological issues: the developmental psychology of young learners, and social-psychological insights into ethnic, cultural identity. Methodological decisions need to be taken in a psychological context of this kind as well as with a view to what learners will find attractive. The resulting influence on materials selection needs to be seen in the light of the proposed aims, and the evaluative criteria of realistic representativeness, ideological critique and so on. The consequence will inevitably be compromise, but compromise reached in the fullest cognisance of all the factors.

Let us make a distinction between 'technique' and 'method' as a means of clarifying how much progress has been made. Ultimately the distinction will be dropped because it could be counter-productive, but initially it will help identify progress towards a methodology, by which is meant a rationale for certain teaching methods explaining them in terms of desired psychological processes. Techniques, on the other hand, are teaching devices whose justification may be solely intuitive or indeed lacking any credible rationale in psychological terms. In the absence of a fully developed methodology, however, intuitive techniques may be equally valid and ultimately absorbed into a methodology. Eventually a model of cultural studies teaching will involve a link between the techniques and methods described in this section and the psychological literature described earlier.

A very useful description of current practice is to be found in an edition of *Études de Linguistique Appliquée* (1982) where a number of authors describe practice in teacher training, in secondary education, in France, Britain and the USA. Knox (1982: 20) sums up much current practice: 'Si travailler ainsi relève encore du bricolage, c'est ainsi à l'image de notre activité dans son ensemble', and calls for more help for teachers in materials, methods and access. It is also symptomatic that articles by Starkey and Talbot both refer to the use of documentation drawn from the press, and implicitly are concerned with techniques for encouraging students to become well informed about the country, a necessary but not sufficient aim in the views of many writers cited elsewhere in this review. A more recent anthology, Valdes (1986), gives an overview of work in the United States. It contains discussion of learning theories developed mainly by language teachers and linguists, and discussions of different kinds of teaching situation in which cultural learning is appropriate. It does not amount, however, to a coherent methodology and remains focused on North American literature.

More psychologically based discussions of methods are found in Baumgratz & Neumann (1980) and in Triandis (1975). The former base their argument on the notion of comparison of phenomena within a higher order framework of comparability: phenomena can be compared only if they can be subsumed under some higher order conceptual system within which they have some traits in common. This requires presentation of phenomena within structures and not atomistically, as we also saw Andersen & Risager and others demanding from a sociological viewpoint.

> Einzelfakten sind als solche ohne Bedeutung. Es geht beim Vergleich um das Aufdecken von Beziehungsverhältnissen innerhalb gesellschaft- licher Teilbereiche oder zwischen gesellschaftlichen Teilbereichen, die auf der Folie der Verhältnisse im eigenen Land untersucht werden.
> (Baumgratz & Neumann, 1980: 164)

They base their account on Vygotskian psychology, and claim that this psychological process creates a distance towards social practices and the awareness that they are historically determined and susceptible of change. Here is a close link with the political, emancipatory aim for cultural studies. Baumgratz & Neumann (1980) also recommend use of texts from the media, and suggest that documents from the home and foreign culture should be deliberately juxtaposed. This leads them to say that the mother tongue must be used in cultural studies, which in turn signifies an uncoupling of cultural and linguistic progression.

Triandis (1975) is not concerned directly with language teaching but with helping individuals to function successfully in another culture, 'inter- cultural relations'. His psychological theory is taken from work on psycho- logical differentiation: 'there are two kinds of people: those who perceive the world wholistically without differentiation of figure and ground, and those who discriminate, analyze, and differentiate' (1975: 61). He extends this concept to degrees and kinds of differentiation made in different cultures and extrapolates that people from two cultures which make similar differentiations in, for example, social relationships, will find it easier to establish good relationships. Where this is not the case, individuals can be trained to perceive the different norms and distinctions made in a particular culture; this kind of approach is similar to work on cultural-specific normal expectancies (Hundeide, 1985) and schemata (Rumelhart, 1980) which are taken up in Chapters 3 and 6. Triandis describes a kind of case-study approach, where learners are presented with a case where two people fail to understand each other and are then offered a number of explanations and gradually acquire the new distinctions. Göhring (1975) has a discussion of comparable work with foreign students in Germany. This and similar approaches discussed by Triandis may well be transferable to secondary schools.

The notion of comparison underlies Triandis' and Göhring's suggestions as it does Baumgratz & Neumann's. The link with Contrastive Analysis (Lado, 1957) is obvious, and Andersen & Risager suggest it should be used also as a means of drawing on the learner's own experience and creating an awareness of 'the relationship between conditions of life and consciousness' (1981: 32). They add a different view of the significance of differentiation in proposing a 'cyclic approach': 'from the earliest stage, the content provides the learner with some concepts and categories that are used during the whole language course, but in a more and more differentiated manner, going from rather simple to more complex social structures' (1981: 32). They suggest that concrete speech situations should be at the heart of any material, but should be accompanied by social information 'stressing the productivity of the linguistic and social categories illustrated' (1981: 35). This leads them, like Baumgratz & Neumann, to recommend the use of the mother tongue, at least in the early stages.

Descriptions of techniques are more common and comparison is a frequent element. Visage (1982) criticises French textbook views of Anglo-American culture—as do Poirier & Rosselin (1982)—and describes how she got her students in the USA to describe their own view of their culture which then served as material for teaching French students. Ehnert, Londeix, Roberts & Rutherford (1981) give an example of contrastive materials on the theme of food and drink in French, German and English. Huhn (1978), as a result of his criteria for evaluating materials, suggests that cultural studies texts should be read critically, looking for ideological and biased viewpoint, 'relativising' the text, rather than allowing it to be the sole source of information. Loveday (1982), Valdman (1966) and Seelye (1974) also have discussions of techniques. Seelye's purpose is to enable students to behave appropriately in a foreign culture, and he bases his work on Maslow's model of human needs. Valdes' (1986) anthology contains six articles described as 'classroom applications' some of which share the general orientation of noticing behavioural differences and learning how to adapt to and accept them, producing the same behaviour where necessary. Others put more emphasis on finding interesting materials—from newspapers or literature—to convey accurate information.

Perhaps the most satisfactory conclusion to this discussion of materials and methods is to find a textbook which exemplifies many of the ideas and principles discussed above. Given the relevance of social anthropology in the analysis of culture it is not surprising to find an anthropologist providing an interesting textbook significantly entitled *As Others See Us*. Hurman (1977) presents pupils with a progressive series of materials and didactic questions which introduces them to fundamental concepts such as stereotype, by starting with the pupils' own world and comparing their view of it with others' reported views. The textbook was piloted in secondary schools in England and as a concrete example of anthropological insights presented to children and young people it appears to be unique, although some other efforts to introduce social anthropology into the British secondary school curriculum have been made (Street, 1987, personal communication).

Conclusion

A number of simple points arise from this survey, which is not exhaustive but deals with representative work:

— despite a wide range of writings, cultural studies lacks direction and fails to attract serious attention, particularly in the Anglo-Saxon world, and consequently lacks status
— existing research is mainly exploratory and theoretical, dealing with concept definition, delimitation of the field of interest and discussion of aims and purposes
— theorists draw on a wider range of academic disciplines than those to which language teachers are usually exposed
— what empirical research and development does exist is usually on a small scale, often arising out of teachers' individual practice, without reference to theory, and concerned with outcomes rather than processes of teaching and learning.

On the one hand this is a picture of a subject under development, looking for a theoretical framework to give it direction. On the other hand, the literature reveals a considerable knowledge and experience of teaching cultural studies within the traditions of foreign language teaching. The task for the future is to improve the situation by bringing together the theory and the practical experience, by theoretically well-founded empirical research.

5 Analysing, Describing and Understanding a Foreign Culture

The emphasis of Chapter 3 lay in the argument that language study and cultural study are closely associated. In this chapter, the emphasis will be on a closer investigation of how cultural study might be possible, how a foreign culture might be accessible to foreign language learners. We begin with questions of delimitation and analysis of the object of study before turning to the problem of access.

Definitions of 'culture' particularly in anthropology are notoriously difficult, as Kaplan & Manners point out (1972: 3): '*Culture* is admittedly an omnibus term. Many investigators have suggested that it is too omnibus to be useful as an analytic tool.' Yet 'culture' is as good a label as any for the overall phenomenon or system of meanings within which sub-systems of social structure, technology, art and so on exist and interconnect. Secondly, 'culture' is a word which has wide and unproblematic circulation outside anthropological literature. Williams (1965: 57) refers to these in his definition:

> There are three general categories in the definition of culture. There is, first, the 'ideal' in which culture is a state or process of human perfection, in terms of certain universal values . . . Then, second, there is the 'documentary' in which culture is the body of intellectual and imaginative work, in which, in a detailed way, human thought and experience are variously recorded. The analysis of culture, from such a definition, is the activity of criticism . . . Finally, third, there is a 'social' definition of culture, in which culture is a description of a particular way of life, which expresses certain meanings and values not only in art and learning but also in institutions and ordinary behaviour.

It is the second of these, and especially the literature element of it, which is usually taught in foreign languages in the later stages of secondary education and in much of higher education, although some change to incorporating aspects of the third definition is evident, for example in polytechnics in the United Kingdom. Writing as an anthropologist Leach (1982: 43) is dealing with the third category in more detail when he writes:

> Almost all empirical societies (i.e. political units which are territorially delimited) are socially stratified ... and each stratum in the system is marked by its own distinctive cultural attributes—linguistic images, manners, styles of food, housing etc.... But not only is there no uniformity in symbolic usage throughout any one society but the cultural differentia that are thus employed are highly unstable over time, as our concept of 'fashion' clearly shows.

There are distinctions to be made within society, and over time, and Leach warns that any 'découpage' of cultural traits or separation of one culture from another within a society is probably more in the eye of the observer than in the complex, over-lapping systems of the society as it in fact exists.

Williams' and Leach's accounts have in common a view of culture as expression of meaning, Leach pointing out that the artefacts used as symbols of meanings are available for different uses by different sections of a society and that the usage is not fixed and stable.

The conception of culture as beliefs, values, meanings is one which is relatively recent. D'Andrade semi-humorously attributes the change to an afternoon in 1957:

> We went from 'let's try to look at behaviour and describe it' to 'let's try to look at ideas'. Now, how you were to look at ideas was a bit of a problem—and some people said 'Well, look at language.' That notion, that you look at idea systems, was extremely general in the social sciences. On, I think, the same afternoon in 1957 you have papers by Chomsky and Miller and, in anthropology, Ward Goodenough. All signal an end to the era of 'Let's look at people's behaviour and see what they do.'
> (quoted in Schweder & LeVine, 1984: 7)

Goodenough's widely cited definition runs as follows (1964: 36):

> A society's culture consists of whatever it is one has to know or believe in order to operate in a manner acceptable to its members. Culture is not a natural phenomenon; it does not consist of things, people's

behaviour or emotions. It is rather an organization of these things. It is the form of things that people have in mind, their models of perceiving, relating, and otherwise interpreting them.

Culture is therefore knowledge, but it is knowledge which is shared and negotiated between people, belonging to all of them and not being idiosyncratic to any single one. Geertz's influential formulation stresses the systematic and inherited nature of the knowledge. Culture is 'an historically transmitted pattern of meanings embodied in symbols, a system of inherited conceptions expressed in a symbolic form by means of which men communicate, perpetuate and develop their knowledge about attitudes towards life' (Geertz, 1975: 89). Much of that knowledge is symbolically expressed in artefacts and behaviours and is formulated as rules, norms, expectations, as moral and legal codes, as proverbs, as parental injunctions to children; but much of it is tacit, scarcely conscious until someone does the unexpected (Hundeide, 1985). Taylor argues that there is a range of meanings—some formulated, some not—which are more than shared in the sense of an individual having a belief which another individual also has. The meanings are part of social reality, constitutive of the practices of social reality:

> The meanings and norms implicit in these practices are not just in the minds of the actors but are out there in the practices themselves, practices which cannot be conceived as a set of individual actions, but which are essentially modes of social relation, of mutual action. (Taylor, 1971: 27)

This is the pattern or web of cultural meanings within which, in Geertz's view, individuals live. Taylor gives the example of 'negotiations'. Actions of individuals are recognised as 'negotiating', 'breaking off negotiations', 'making an offer' because they are perceived as conforming to norms which constitute the activity; the norms are not just inside the individual's head, they are inter-subjective meanings. He then identifies a further range of meanings which are also part of social reality: 'common meanings' are in a sense artefacts embodying the culture:

> By these I mean notions of what is significant, which are not just shared in the sense that everyone has them, but are also common in the sense of being in the common reference world . . .

His example here is the notion of the survival of a national identity as francophones, which is a 'common meaning' for Quebecois. He then goes on to link common meanings with community (1971: 30):

> Common meanings are the basis of community. Intersubjective meaning gives a people a common language to talk about social reality

and a common understanding of certain norms, but only with common meanings does this common reference world contain significant common actions, celebrations and feelings. These are the objects in the world that everybody shares. This is what makes community.

Thus, particularly effectively through the use of the word 'object' in the penultimate sentence, Taylor has identified another kind of artefact alongside those in the physical world, such as clothing or national flags and those which are representations of ideas, such as poems or folk-songs. One of the cultural objects of the Quebecois which any definition or analysis must capture is the common meaning 'the survival of national identity as francophones'. That object must be described just as much as the physical objects or patterns of behaviour which embody Quebecois culture.

The first kind of shared meaning identified by Taylor can be described in terms of 'constitutive rules', descriptive rules of how people in a given society agree on their shared meanings. Citing Searle, D'Andrade (1984: 91) explains how marriage exists within American culture:

> Marriage is a part of American culture in that there is a constitutive system of rules that individuals know, which are intersubjectively shared and adhered to. Enactment of certain behaviour counts in certain contexts as 'getting married', and once married, certain obligations and commitments are incurred. Marriage is a culturally created entity—*an entity created by the social agreement that something counts as that entity*. To agree that something will count as something else is more than simply knowing about it, although knowing about it is a necessary precondition. The *agreement* that something counts as something else involves the *adherence* of a group of people to a *constitutive rule* and to the entailments incurred by the application of the rule.
> [Author's own emphasis]

In this view of culture, then, the mere observation of behaviour is not simply rejected but is pointless unless the actors' agreements about the meaning of the behaviour are part of the account. Similarly, the artefacts which are used as part of the behaviour and to symbolise the meanings, such as the marriage ring or wedding dress or the church building, can only be properly comprehended in the whole system of meanings which are inherent in the behaviour of, for example, the marriage ceremony.

Societal institutions, too, carry cultural meanings. They can be described in terms of observable behaviour; for example the election of members of parliament can be described in terms of what electors do on certain dates, how votes are counted and winners declared. The cultural significance of these behaviours only becomes clear when electors' beliefs about the meanings of their actions are formulated. If an individual were simply to carry out the action of putting a cross on a ballot paper and inserting the paper in a box, he would not be voting unless he knew that the agreed significance of his actions was describable in terms of constitutive rules.

In the context of foreign language teaching, therefore, to describe the behaviours, the artefacts, the institutions of a foreign culture is inadequate. It is to remain stuck in the behaviourism of pre-1957. It is necessary to give an account of the significance of behaviours, artefacts and institutions in terms of the culturally agreed meanings which they embody, of which they are realisations. Thus when we begin to analyse and describe the culture associated with a particular foreign language, we need to bear the following points in mind.

In any one culture—which in complex societies is an abstraction from the social reality of one substratum—we should be looking at the meanings of the actions and the artefacts of individuals or groups of individuals. The artefacts are products of and symbols for meaningful actions and are therefore themselves meaningful. The actions acquire their meaning from the norms or constitutive rules which are recognised and agreed by all and which, independently of individuals, are part of social reality; norms and expectations constitute social reality, being inter-subjective meanings. In a sense they are objects in social reality just as much as the artefacts which result from and symbolise them. In particular there is a class of meanings in social reality which are objects apropos of which individuals feel a sense of community: common meanings. Common meanings are therefore fundamental artefacts of a culture. Artefacts in the physical world, whether from traditional art forms or from culinary or sartorial styles, are the tangible products and symbols which are infused with the meanings of the culture. Artefacts of literature, music and the like are the expressions both of the idiosyncratic meanings of individuals and also of the systems of meaning which individuals share.

It is evident that the agreement and formulation of cultural meaning is carried out in the language of the community. Language has a special role to play—supplemented by other forms of communication, notably music and painting—and the special role of language is of course of particular interest to the foreign language teacher as was argued in Chapter 3. In discussing the question of the interpretation of meaningful actions, Taylor considers the issue of whether a textual account of action can properly express the meaning of the action when action and text are two different terms of comparison. He argues that the two terms are not independent of each other (1971: 15):

> The field of meanings in which a given situation can find its place is bound up with the semantic field of the terms characterizing these meanings and the related feelings, desires, predicaments.

The relationship is, as Taylor points out, not a simple one, but suffice it for the moment to say that language differs from other symbolic systems in that it always refers beyond itself to other symbols and phenomena, it has a meta-function, and thus takes up a key position in culture. Inter-subjective meanings are an integral part of societal institutions; they are what makes an action carried out within the framework of the institution meaningful. They are formulated in varying degrees of explicitness. Thus the legal system can only function by virtue of the highly explicit agreed definitions of what is lawful or not, agreed and formulated in a highly explicit code. Common meanings, shared beliefs, aspirations and perceptions, are dependent on the presence of inter-subjective meanings but are not likely to be tied to any one societal institution. They may be articulated dimly and implicitly in actions and symbols, such as practices of inviting friends and strangers into one's home or styles of house-building which reinforce or break down privacy. They may be articulated most explicitly in one kind of cultural artefact: what Williams calls 'documentary', the products of artists and craftsmen. Some significant common meanings of American society are articulated in Arthur Miller's *Death of a Salesman*. Lucien Goldmann's analysis of Racine's work (1956) elucidates some of the common meanings of parts of seventeenth-century French society: the ideology present in Racine's plays. The less explicitly formulated meanings of ordinary life of one part of British society were captured in Richard Hoggart's account of working class people (1957). Social anthropologists are of course the scholars who are most concerned with this latter kind of analysis, often labelled cognitive anthropology. The meanings in the former kind of work are elucidated by literary critics.

Common and inter-subjective meanings exist independently of given individuals, they are the objects produced by the group. They are not accessible in a pure form but are inherent in the expectations of the group as to 'rational' behaviour, and in the artefacts which symbolise and are expressions of the meanings of that behaviour. There are thus two potential starting points for analysis: behaviour—including in particular linguistic behaviour—and artefacts and symbols. Because language has a special relationship to common and inter-subjective meanings, it is likely to provide the best starting point. But because linguistic behaviour does not exist independently of other behaviour, analysis has to be of language in the context of other symbols. The purpose of analysis is to provide a reading of the behaviour and associated artefacts which includes a formulation of the meanings inherent in it. Geertz describes it in a way which will appeal to foreign language teachers trained in literary scholarship (1975: 10):

> Doing ethnography is like trying to read (in the sense of 'construct a reading of') a manuscript—foreign, faded, full of ellipses, incoherencies, suspicious emendations, and tendentious commentaries, but written not in conventional graphs of sound but in transient examples of shaped behaviour.

The reading will itself be expressed in language, an expression which should be explicit, ordered and clear, and thus will often be a contrast to the explicandum. To use language as the expression of analysis is to capitalise on its special relationship with cultural meanings, as I propose to call the web of inter-subjective meanings, common meanings and expectations about behaviour. In short, individuals' experience of cultural meanings is reflected in the semantic of their language. They negotiate and express those meanings above all in their common language. Widdowson (1985: 17) describes this as a shift from symbolic meaning to individual, 'indexical' meanings: 'Whereas then symbolic meanings inhere in the signs themselves, indexical meanings must be achieved by the language user associating them with some relevant aspect of the world outside language, in the situation or in the mind.' The individual user does not usually carry out this procedure alone but as part of the social process of negotiating and acquiring cultural meanings. (The relationship of these to the schemata of knowledge with which individuals interpret their world will be discussed in Chapter 6.)

This is not to say that the negotiations and expressions are clear and complete, but it does mean that clarification through language, through reformulation, development of implications and so on, will still be directly in touch with individuals' experience. The language of interpretation still functions with the same semantic fields, the same lexis and syntax. A reading and interpretation of behaviour and artefacts is in this case still within the same culture; the explicandum and the explicans are essentially of the same world.

For an example of the analysis of culture, we may turn to those interested in cross-cultural psychology. Triandis offers a definition of 'subjective culture' which overlaps with the notion of common meanings: 'By subjective culture we mean a cultural group's characteristic way of perceiving its social environment . . . Subjective culture refers to variables

that are attributes of the cognitive structure of groups of people' (1972: 3).
In his list of dimensions of subjective culture, he provides a number of
categories into which the shared and common meanings of a group may be
placed: associations, attitudes, beliefs, evaluations, categorisations, expectations, memories, opinions, percepts, role perceptions, stereotypes, values.
The illustrative analyses of the notion of subjective culture deal largely with
stereotyping on the basis of experimental investigation. There is, for
example, a comparison of American and Greek culture. Triandis summarises the experimental results under certain thematic headings: national
character, relationships with others, work habits, religious-philosophical
concepts, institutions and social processes, values and disvalues. This is a
useful practical basis for analysis and description.

The question now arises: is it possible for an interpreter from another
culture to understand? Can he translate the explanation of a foreign culture
into his own language and the semantics of his own cultural meanings? Or
must he attempt to use the language of the world to be interpreted, and if
so, can he succeed, can he grasp that language and world? These are the
questions which arise for the foreign language teacher who wishes to help
pupils to understand and hence empathise with the experience of people in a
foreign culture.

Leach, cited above, reminds us that each society has substrata, each
with its own culture, its own world and language. The question of whether
an interpreter from one world can understand the meanings of another
world is pertinent both within one society and from another society. At first
glance, there is the significant difference that one society usually shares
'the same' language. The language consists in fact of dialects, which are
lexically, syntactically and semantically related, but which have their
individual character. The semantic dimension of their character reflects the
particular cultural meanings of the dialect's users. The dialect will coincide
with others in so far as there are shared meanings, but there will be
deviations. An interpreter from one substratum will find in the world of
another substratum some cultural and linguistic meanings which are
familiar, and others which are unfamiliar. In order to understand those
which are unfamiliar—or those which are broadly similar but subtly
different from familiar ones—he will need to make an imaginative leap into
the experience of the individuals of that substratum. He can be helped to
make that leap by interpretations which are more ordered and explicit than
usual. The interpretations which are closer to the semantics of his own
dialect will be most useful to him, a bridge across the gap. The explicitness
and orderedness of the interpretations will be a matter of degree, as will the
proximity to his own dialect. The interpretations may be written directly for

him or they may be linguistic artefacts which members of the substratum have produced as part of their own attempt to understand their culture. An example of the first would be an anthropological ethnography; an example of the second would be a novel in the realist tradition. The novelist writes with the language of his own world and that of his reader. He may comment on and explain the people he describes, but he does so within the traditions to which both he and his reader belong. If the reader is from another culture, whether simply another section of society or from a radically different society, then there is a need for translation, transfer of meanings in one culture to make them comprehensible to a reader living within a different system of meanings. But who is to mediate this transfer, who is to translate the system of meanings? The answer has to be someone who understands the culture of the writer and of the reader, but that is not enough. He must also understand the process by which the reader can be helped to place himself within the cultural meanings of the writer, abandoning temporarily, where necessary, those of his own cultural meanings which clash with and prevent him from seeing the meanings of the other culture. This is the work of the literary critic who writes about foreign literature for readers in his own culture. It is, however, also the work of the social anthropologist who explains a foreign culture to those who have not experienced it. More precisely, Sperber (1985: 10) argues that it is the work of the anthropologist as ethnographer:

> Most anthropologists would be better—and no less honourably— described as ethnographers. They are more interested in specific cultures than in Homo Sapiens's cultural abilities and dispositions, in varieties of human experience than in its variability. Ethnography is an important pursuit in its own right. It answers a legitimate curiosity as to what it is like to belong to another culture, to be Nuer, Tibetan or French—a curiosity which is not so much about facts as about the way these facts are subjectively experienced, and which calls for interpretations rather than mere descriptions.

For the foreign language teacher the issue does not stop at satisfying legitimate curiosity, which he indeed may have first to stimulate; it is also his task to create empathy and understanding. As an educator he has to shake and trouble the complacency of his pupils, to stimulate their curiosity, but also to encourage them to go beyond the dangerous stage of then perceiving the Nuer, the Tibetan or the Frenchman as curious, odd and perhaps disturbing, to use Moscovici's striking comparison (1984: 25): 'the mentally handicapped or people belonging to other cultures are disturbing, because they are like us, and yet not like us; so we may say they are "un-cultural", "barbarian", "irrational" and so on.' It is important that foreign language teachers recognise this potential reaction, incorporate it into their presentation of the foreign culture and take their pupils at least to the stage of tolerance, and preferably to understanding. This is particularly evident with respect to exotic cultures which are very different from our own, where our own rationality is no basis on which to comprehend another (Winch, 1964). It is more subtle and more difficult to grasp with respect to a culture such as the French. Yet because French culture can evoke the same responses (cf. Chapter 7, on pupil interviews) it is all the more important to anticipate them and the potential danger. Tolerance of a culture similar yet subtly different from our own is no less difficult, and empathy with it no less of a challenge than tolerance of or empathy with the exotic.

Tolerance involves acceptance of others, refraining from wishing to destroy them or at least to banish them because they disturb us, a reaction towards the mentally handicapped which is still common in our Western societies. Towards foreign people, tolerance involves, in the contemporary world, willingness to work and live with people who are different, refraining from banishing them from our society as we do in the present, or even waging war upon them, as we have done in the past. Empathy on the other hand, is more demanding. It requires understanding, an activity rather than a passive acceptance; it requires a change of viewpoint which has to be worked towards, engaged with. Von Wright (1971: 28) suggests that this is common to all social scientists, not just the ethnographer, and the implication is that both teacher and pupils have to engage in the procedures of the social scientist:

> The description, and understanding, of social behaviour must employ the same conceptual framework as the social agents themselves. For this reason the social scientist cannot remain an outsider in relation to his object of study in the same sense in which a natural scientist can. *This* is the core of conceptual truth, one could say, in the psychologistic doctrine of 'empathy'. Empathic understanding is not a 'feeling'; it is an ability to participate in a 'form of life'.

The ethnographer differs from the literary critic in that he does not have a text which is available to all his readers. He is not only writing a commentary, he is in a sense creating a text and simultaneously interpreting it. Creating the text, describing the culture has to be, at least initially, in that culture's own terms, for otherwise distortion can enter even before interpretation begins. However, in most cases even the description has to involve translation, in the literal sense of being written in a language other than that of the culture the ethnographer is describing. What difference does it make if he uses the culture's own language?

Let us consider the two possibilities: description (and interpretation) in another language and description (and perhaps also interpretation) in the native language of the culture. Sperber (1985: 11) argues that a description is a special kind of representation and that like all representations it has to be 'adequate to its object':

> a description is a representation which is adequate when it is true. Truth-or-falsity is an exclusive property of propositions. Only utterances convey propositions. Hence descriptions have to be in the form of utterances.

From this he goes on to argue that descriptions are open to evaluation and can be used as scientific evidence. There appears to be an assumption in this argument that only denotative meanings come into play in propositions and their utterance. In so far as this is the case and in so far as we accept that the words of one language can either be directly represented by the words of another or adequately paraphrased and defined, then Sperber's account of descriptions allows for descriptions in a language foreign to the culture in question. Connotative meanings must however be excluded, for through them there arise not just the personal connotations of any reader of the description but, far more significantly, the shared connotations, the cultural connotations which would wrongly colour the description. A statement that, for example, 'West Germans value their democratic tradition' has a different resonance for the West Germans themselves—in the historical connotations of the rise, fall and regeneration of democracy since 1918 and in the contemporary contrast with East Germany—than it has for a British reader with a different history and no equivalent to East Germany. Of the two kinds of connotations—the personal and the cultural—the second can, however, be captured by further descriptive statements about the history and politics of West and East Germany. In principle, then, a description of one culture in the language of another is possible, provided very tight controls are maintained. Yet if we accept von Wright's argument quoted above that 'understanding of social behaviour must employ the same conceptual framework as the social agents themselves', and if we accept that the formulation of concepts in language has inevitable connotative resonance, then the advantages for the person who can read an account of the culture in its own language are immediately evident. However, the advantages are only accessible to someone whose understanding of the language is sufficiently developed.

What then do we mean by sufficiently developed? Ideally, he must abandon the semantics of his own language—and culture—and take up the semantics of the foreign language. This involves what I referred to above as an 'imaginative leap'. His understanding of his own culture is largely inexplicit, unconscious. Cultural meanings guide his actions and much of his thinking even though they are often not immediately accessible. They do not entirely determine his actions and thinking, as his deviations from norms and expectations indicate; but he feels uncomfortable when acting deviantly. That discomfort derives from the fact that he has acquired the meanings through experience which has emotional, affective dimensions, represented in the connotative, affective dimensions of his mother tongue. That experience and the consequent linguistic connotations involve both individual, personal associations and shared, cultural associations. If his acquisition of a foreign culture were similar to his experience of acquiring his own culture—that is, if there were similar or even identical affective dimensions—then his understanding of a foreign culture would be indistinguishable from that of a native. The same applies to language acquisition as a part of the whole process. This cannot, however, be the case. Childhood and psychological development are not repeatable, a truism which nonetheless bears repetition.

However, a substitute for unconscious cultural, and linguistic, competence can be provided through conscious learning, accompanied by an imaginative willingness to abandon temporarily the semantics of his own language and culture. The substitution is not complete; the personal, individual dimension is lacking. Yet there is a sense in which this does not matter. Cultural meanings are objects created by the group. They are created by negotiation and exist independently of any single group member. Each member doubtless has his own interpretation and experience of the meanings, but there is sufficient overlap of understandings for there to be agreement. If the foreigner can apprehend the agreed core of meaning and the shared, cultural connotations, then his lack of an experiential, affective connotation at an individual level is not an insuperable deficiency. It is in this sense possible to learn a foreign language and learn about a foreign culture, using the tools of conscious learning. It remains, however, cerebral, unemotional and an incomplete experience. It can be enriched by experience which is a substitute for the experience of the native, without being identical with it. Where the learning takes place within the target society, rather han in the foreign language classroom, the affective dimension is likely to be fuller and more complex, since the experience of any one aspect of the culture will be inseparable from others, whereas in the classroom an artificial separation is possible and may be desirable. Provided the experience is comparable to that of a native, and not biased by the special nature of being a foreign participant, then empathic understanding, as von Wright calls it, may begin to develop. For the participant begins to perceive the culture from within the conceptual and experiential framework of the native. Yet the individual is unlikely, except in extreme cases, to abandon his own framework more than temporarily. There is likely to be a constant comparison, shifting to and fro between the two frameworks. This comparative element is not unknown to the natives of the culture, although from a different viewpoint and for different reasons.

Barth (1969) points out that to treat cultures as if they were isolated from each other is to miss a significant dimension. Cultures and cultural or ethnic groups usually live in contact with others. In order to maintain identity and separateness, certain cultural phenomena are emphasised by the group to contrast with and mark a boundary *vis-à-vis* other groups. Cohen supports and develops Barth's argument in his analysis of 'locality' in British rural cultures. He suggests that locality—the sense of belonging to a particular geographical area—is, like ethnicity, an expression of culture. This allows him to state 'a more general principle: that people become aware of their culture when they stand at its boundaries' (1982: 3), which could just as well be a description of foreign language learning. Barth goes on to argue that cultural analysis should be concerned initially with boundaries—which may be realised by different phenomena at different times—rather than with the cultural stuff within those boundaries. One advantage of this approach is that it reveals how a group presents itself to others, which phenomena it chooses to emphasise and which to ignore. In this sense the insider's own account of his culture comes to the fore. Where cultures have much in common and are perhaps historically related—as is the case in Western Europe—the need to focus on boundary phenomena in order to express individuality is just as strong as between non-related cultures and will reveal significant differences between cultures as they are experienced from the inside. This helps to avoid the stereotyping of differences from the outside. On the other hand, the very notion of selection of boundary phenomena means that there are other phenomena which are part of experience and which must not be forgotten in a description of a culture; but let us consider first the boundary phenomena.

It was argued above that some phenomena are explicit and conscious, others not; there are tangible artefacts and behaviours and less tangible common meanings. It is the more tangible which will be most accessible to consciousness and most prominent as boundary markers. Barth (1969: 14) distinguishes two levels:

> The cultural contents of ethnic dichotomies would seem analytically to be of two orders: (i) overt signals or signs—the diacritical features that people look for and exhibit to show identity, often such features as

dress, language, house-form, or general style of life, and (ii) basic value orientations: the standards of morality and excellence by which performance is judged.

Such 'value orientations' have the ontological status of Taylor's 'common meanings'. As Barth points out, a descriptive listing by an observer of phenomena of both kinds would not necessarily include or isolate those chosen by the group itself to emphasise its identity. There is no principled basis for prediction of which will be considered by the group as significant. Barth's analysis is particularly welcome in a comparative approach which could be used for teaching. It helps to avoid the stereotyping of another culture from a standpoint within one's own where the stereotype arises in part from the bias created by one's own boundary phenomena. A view conditioned by one's own boundary phenomena will tend to pick out the direct contrasts in the other culture which may not be considered at all significant by the members of that culture themselves.

Cohen, however, enters a caveat which takes us back to non-boundary phenomena. Accepting Geertz's interpretivist view of culture as a web of meaning of great complexity, he suggests that 'when a community presents itself to the outside world (as when any level of society engages with another) it simplifies its message and its character down to the barest of essentials' (Cohen, 1982: 8). The lived experience of all cultural identity is not so much in the boundary phenomena, whose markedness is their fundamental characteristic, but in the mundane, unmarked practices of everyday life. Boundary-marking dichotomies are necessary in situations of contact with other cultures, and particularly necessary when the local or ethnic culture is under threat from larger societal groupings. The value of accounts of sections or sub-groups of complex Western societies is to emphasise that the tendency to homogenise 'British' or 'French' culture by reference to national boundary phenomena distorts the experience of cultural identity which 'British' or 'French' people really have. This is not to suggest there is no such thing as 'British' identity, but rather that any individual may choose at any given moment and for reasons arising from particular situations to identify as belonging to a particular village, region or nation, not to mention professional, familial and other dimensions of identity. In foreign language teaching learners are presented with national identities and are thereby implicitly encouraged to respond in terms of their own national identity. The problem which arises in such an emphasis is that the higher the level, the more distant the experiential meaning of culture of the individual person. The tendency to present a simplified account of a culture to the outside world in boundary-marking terms is compounded by the simplifications of high level identity. (Cohen (1982: 10) argues that:

> with each 'ascending' level I increasingly simplify (and thereby misrepresent) the message about myself. At each descending level I present myself through increasingly informed and complex pictures. It should therefore be recognised that 'belonging to locality', far from being a parochial triviality, is very much more of a cultural reality than is association with gross region or nation.

This argument raises problems for foreign language teaching which will be addressed below.

What now is the answer to the question which has guided the argument so far? Is it possible to understand a foreign culture? The answer must be a qualified yes. In so far as language is part of culture and can capture cultural meanings and experiences (but can it capture all, including those expressed in music and the visual arts?) then it is possible to interpret and describe a culture in its language. The language holds the culture through the denotations and connotations of its semantics. The question is then how successfully the culture can be described in another language. In principle it is possible through utterances of descriptive propositions which capture shared cultural meanings. There exists, however, an association of personal experiences and emotions with the acquisition of shared, cultural meanings. In this respect the individual cannot hope to repeat in his own language the experience of an individual in the culture under description. A similar problem arises if the individual attempts to understand the other culture through the foreign language; the personal, affective dimension will be lacking. The lack can be made up only in part, as there are some experiences, of childhood in particular, which are not repeatable for the adolescent or adult. On the other hand, direct experience of the foreign culture can enrich the description of culturally shared meanings and connotations by acquisition of personal associations in the flux of complex interactions of cultural meanings.

Let us now consider how the foregoing discussion might impinge on the foreign language classroom. As argued from a different starting point in Chapter 3, the logic of the argument here indicates the unsurprising conclusion that language and culture should be learnt in an integral manner. That is, an aspect of culture—whether tangible artefact or shared, cultural meaning—should be approached through the language items which refer to or express it. To attempt to refer to or express it in the learners' native language, though not impossible, is less desirable than to do so in the foreign language. For not only is the imaginative leap required a valuable educational experience, but also the advantages for language learning evident in bilingual education may be reaped. The danger that the foreign language is assimilated to the native language and with it the foreign culture—i.e. that it is perceived as a one-to-one code of the native language—is of course continuously present. In this case the imaginative leap does not take place and the educational value is undermined. But this is nothing new in foreign language teaching and the emphasis on cultural learning may reduce this problem, whereas over-emphasis of language as system separate from its culture, by turning the attention away from meaning, frequently encourages the assimilation process.

Having established this first conclusion, there are two directions from which to approach classroom practice: by starting afresh and producing teaching material and practice from the theoretical basis or by critique and modification of existing material and practice in the light of theory. We shall sketch out how each approach might be attempted. Although the complications such as level of learning involved, age and development of learners, and methodology will be borne in mind, we shall not attempt to take rigorous account of all these dimensions at this exploratory stage.

In order to have a starting point for a theory-generated discussion which relates directly to practice let us work with two broad categories of 'elementary' and 'advanced' learners of French in English schools—in secondary education terms 11- to 13- and 16- to 18-year-olds. The overriding issue is the decision as to what is to be taught, what cultural content is to be selected for presentation to the learners and how the presentation is to be incorporated into language teaching as a whole. We know that the French language is associated with a number of countries and that within each national society there are many subdivisions or substrata. The selection of one country rather than another may be governed by practical questions of geographical proximity and the opportunity to introduce first-hand experience of the culture into the course. There is also the possibility of introducing other countries and cultures at different stages in the course—perhaps linked through the cultural concept of '*la Francophonie*'.

On the assumption that France is selected first, it is evident enough that the complexity of an advanced, industrialised society requires further choices to be made. One possibility is to choose one substratum and to represent part of its culture. This has been the usual approach in textbooks, leading to a partial view of the way of life of a particular sphere of French society, represented by the traditional textbook family. The problem of selecting just one family and the consequent limitations have been recognised in more recent textbooks and a wider selection has been introduced. This has led to the introduction of more substrata and, sometimes, to a greater breadth of selection from their way of life, for example more attention to work as well as leisure. Nonetheless the approach remains intrinsically the same: selection of what are intended to be figures and events which, when added together, represent the whole society and culture. The notion of representation involved here is probably intuitive, based on concepts of the number of people in the same socio-economic categories as the textbook figures and the frequency of the events they experience. Added to this are considerations of what is different from the learners' culture and what they might experience themselves as non-native visitors to the country.

An alternative to this 'arithmetical' concept of representation is suggested by Barth's emphasis, already mentioned above, on self-presentation and the creation by ethnic groups of boundaries which separate them from other groups. These boundaries would tend in the first instance to be marked overtly by what Barth calls the diacritical features such as dress or housing, but their significance depends on their symbolising cultural meanings, particularly those which are the basis of a community, making it different from others. The link between the symbols and the common meanings can be made through language, through descriptive propositions in the language of the culture, made by a member of the culture. This has the advantage of presenting cultural phenomena from within the semantics of the language, reducing the danger of assimilation to the language and culture of the learner which the outsider's perspective of the non-native visitor encourages. In a complex society, however, individuals belong to more than one group. They may, for example, identify as Alsaciens and not Parisiens, as Meridionaux and not from le Nord, as town and not country dwellers, as working class and not middle class, as French and not Belgian, as belonging to *la Francophonie* and not English-speaking, as European and not Asians and so on. Which of these identities is uppermost at any given moment will depend on the circumstances of where one is living, whom one is speaking to, what one is speaking about. The Alsacien in Paris feels his Alsacien identity more strongly than in Strasbourg. When on holiday in the Midi, he feels more strongly his Northern identity; when speaking to English people his French identity is dominant. Each of these identities would be symbolised differently and embodied in a different set of statements.

This kind of analysis allows the substrata to be identified and also points to criteria for selection. For, at an elementary learner level, the linguistically and culturally dominant identity of the learners meeting a foreign language for the first time is likely to be their national language identity: their Englishness, assuming they are learning French in an English secondary school. What they confront is a national language identity in the figures they meet in textbooks and the people they meet on visits. It is appropriate therefore to confront them with that national language identity not as the outsider perceives it but as the insider presents it, an insider, moreover, who is of similar age to themselves. Simplistically and summarily, the learners should confront French 11- to 13-year-olds explaining and describing to them what being French is like. This is not to suggest, of course, that a French 12-year-old can explicate his cultural identity in a series of descriptive statements. The practical question for the textbook writer and the teacher is how to acquire an account from native speakers which can be made accessible to learners through explication and pedagogic techniques.

At an advanced level, the process of analysis of the foreign and the native culture and identity of the learners begun through the confrontation with the national identity should lead to a greater subtlety of perspective. At this level, the point at issue will be how individuals present themselves to others within their national culture: how Alsaciens present themselves to Parisiens and vice versa, for example. This will not lead necessarily to a comprehensive view and experience of the whole culture, but this is not a disadvantage in curriculum development terms. For, as was argued in Chapter 3, the subject 'Cultural Studies' should be a process guided by the principles of an academic discipline, not a pre-determined series of behavioural objectives to be mastered or a comprehensive account of a whole culture to be experienced. In the course of seeing and studying the culture from one viewpoint, being exposed to one part of the whole, learners will begin to understand the principles of social study in accordance with which their independent experience of other parts of the culture may develop.

The same point applies when we return to the elementary level. There is here, too, an impossible task of comprehensive cover of the self-presentation of being French. It is inevitable that even within that dimension of national identity some selection has to take place. Because of the age of the learners, it is important to have some concrete focus to the selection, as well as conforming to the principles of the underlying discipline. We are thus looking for a description by a native speaker of an artefact which carries significant meanings and which is perceived by members of the society as a boundary marker of their identity *vis-à-vis* other nationalities. For example, food is often chosen by textbook writers as a focus and could well be selected by a native speaker—perhaps in part because French people are aware of other people's perceptions of France: fashion, riviera and haute cuisine; and in part because the preparation of food is a part of the self-presentation of national identity. Rather than a textbook presentation from the outsider's point of view, however, we need an insider account which is the kind of factual description which can be made to reveal the common meanings attached to the preparation and consumption of food. Such common meanings are, however, not necessarily clearly formulated in the native speaker consciousness—particularly of younger people—and part of the pedagogic problem-field is to elicit and explicate meanings as well as to make them accessible to learners in a linguistic form which is within their learner competence in the foreign language. This is indeed a considerable problem at an elementary stage. At an advanced level the principles of focus selection and presentation remain the same, and the difficulties of access will diminish. At an advanced level, however, the shift to presentation of identities within the national boundaries may lead to less focus on artefacts and more emphasis on increasingly subtle cultural distinctions formulated in correspondingly subtle linguistic expression. For example, it is currently common practice to introduce advanced learners to social and economic problems by selecting articles from prominent newspapers and journals. Rather than the outsider approach to issues such as decentralisation—an approach which is implicit in the isolation of one article from one kind of national newspaper—it would be important to have insider accounts from a regional viewpoint (Mariet, 1985) where the shared meanings and values vis-à-vis the centre could be made accessible to advanced learners. Another example might be a regional approach to the question of food. Refining the elementary approach, this would involve accounts of the place of food in regional identity, perhaps in different social classes, again through insider accounts which might be juxtaposed and compared in order to make the underlying shared meanings accessible to the outsider, to the advanced learner. All of this points quite clearly to the need for 'authentic' teaching material, where the current emphasis on authenticity for linguistic reasons is reinforced and made more problematic by these criteria of cultural self-presentation.

The kind of self-presentation suggested here would give learners a conscious, ordered series of insights into the system of meanings which underlie the sense of national community, at elementary level, and regional community, at advanced level. On the other hand the simplifications and misrepresentations which arise from 'high level identities', to use Cohen's terminology, are still inherent in this approach. The ideal would be that learners should share the experience of culture in the mundane detail of daily practices. In this way, too, learners would have not simply a cognitive understanding of the foreign culture but would be offered an affective, experiential learning comparable to that of the native or to learners' experience of their own cultural identity. This would be truly an expansion of learners' experience in a fundamentally developmental sense and would make the educational value of language and culture learning apparent to all.

How then is the complexity of cultural experience to be made accessible to language learners, for it is a complexity which cannot be caught easily or entirely by propositional description? Geertz's (1975) notion of 'thick description' and of constructing a reading of a foreign culture offers a way of linking the detail of locality and daily life with the overall meanings of a culture. His account of Moroccan shepherding practices is an excellent illustration. Yet reading an ethnographic account is like reading a critical analysis of a novel or a film. It is a valuable and essential aid to understanding which nonetheless invites the reader to look beyond it to the object described. In ethnographic work, the writer attempts to provide this opportunity by descriptions, photographs and films. In literary or film criticism, the object is publicly available for readers or filmgoers to experience directly. In foreign language teaching the object has traditionally been made available indirectly through descriptions, pictures and the use of realist literature as a mirror of the foreign society. The similar role which realist films might play, especially for young learners, has not been fully recognised. In more recent times, of course, the object of description has become much more directly accessible through increase in travel opportunities.

The advantages of direct experience or even of the vicarious presentation through realist films or novels are twofold. First, the complexity of cultural experience which critical analysis or ethnography cannot capture or relay to learners, is available to them in the detail of daily life. Second, learners can become affectively as well as cognitively involved in their experience of the foreign culture's complexity in ways which ethnographers' accounts or teachers' anecdotes cannot simulate. However, these advantages are only potential and cannot be taken for granted without the help and contribution of the interpreter and critic— ethnographer or teacher, or rather teacher as ethnographer. For, as will be argued in Chapter 6, learners may otherwise easily overlook and assimilate the new cultural experience to existing concepts and interpretations.

In practical terms, the possibilities of direct experience would have influence on the selection of material and insider viewpoint outlined above. In simplistic ways this already happens in those textbooks which set their scene in Paris or the Channel ports because these are easy to reach with groups of school pupils. In the present argument, the issue is more complex. If, for example, the form of the direct experience of the culture were to be a week's visit to a town in Normandy for pupils in the second year of French learning—to take an illustration from actual practice—then the self-presentation of national identity would have to be compared with the regional and local identity. For the pupils would in that week meet national, regional and local symbols of identity, of cultural meanings, and would experience above all the minutiae of local culture. The preparation of materials to be studied in advance would have to take this into account, and would be developed during the week's visit where with the help of teachers' interpretations pupils would experience the three dimensions as a complex whole, impinging as much on their emotions as upon their cognitive understanding.

In conclusion let us now consider current practice in the light of this account of description of and access to another culture. In general, the integration of language and culture teaching central to the argument of this chapter is most nearly realised in advanced classes. In traditional British university courses the methods of language teaching based on the translation of literary texts and comparison of literary registers in two languages—whatever their merits in language learning terms—focus learners' attention on the nuances of linguistic meaning which are ultimately realisations of cultural meanings. There is, of course, no attempt at comprehensive coverage and indeed contemporary culture often has a low priority, but the methods do at least provide one way of creating in learners the required cultural sensitivity. These methods are based on the well-founded assumption that literary texts embody the relationship of all linguistic texts to cultural meanings but do so in a more concentrated, and therefore more accessible and rewarding form. That many learners then go on to turn these methods solely to the study of the uniqueness of each author of established literature rather than considering also the representativeness of authors of the society in which they lived is for our purposes regrettable, even though defensible within certain canons of critical theory.

In the British education system, however, such learners are a tiny minority of all those who begin to learn a foreign language, for after three or four years most pupils give up language learning. Although in other European countries most pupils continue for longer periods, five or six years or more, the question of an integrated pedagogy of language and culture in the early stages is nonetheless important and equally problematic. There are several factors which create the problem, not all of them linguistic. Pupils of 11 to 13 years of age learning a language from the beginning are faced with the problem of being able to express only simplified meanings which bear little relation to the stage of socialisation and acquisition of cultural meanings they have reached. On the other hand they have not reached a stage of full, adult cultural competence in their own culture, whereas the foreign culture is often analysed and interpreted in adult terms, at least by social anthropologists and other non-language teachers engaged in cultural study. In short the pupils are linguistically far behind their peers in the foreign culture and, second, the cultural analysis available is ahead of the cultural competence of even those foreign peers. The obvious solution of concentrating on linguistic competence teaching until pupils begin to approach their peers' competence, and then re-analysing the culture in terms of the competence of adolescents will not, of course, do. In three or even five years of normal secondary school teaching, pupils will not catch up sufficiently on native speaker peers and are simultaneously developing in their own cultural competence and outstripping the kind of analysis they might have been exposed to as 11- or 12-year-olds. Thus the problem appears intractable and the emphasis by those attempting new approaches to Cultural Studies on materials and methods for advanced learners is probably an indication of the lack of solutions to this major problem. As we saw in Chapter 4, those few researchers who do consider the younger or more elementary learners are prepared to suggest that learners' native language be used (Andersen & Risager, 1981: Baumgratz & Neumann, 1980).

I do not propose a surprise ending to this chapter in the form of a panacea. The issue of socialisation and age-dependent development within the home culture points rather to the need for consideration of the psychological analysis of cultural competence, and it is to this that we turn in the following chapter.

6 Psychological Dimensions of Cultural Studies Learning

The purpose of this chapter is to consider what psychological effect and changes might be expected and encouraged in pupils who learn about a foreign culture. Let it be said from the outset that this is an area which is still in its initial stages of development. Keller (1983b) and Buttjes (1982) represent the state of discussion in the German literature. Acton & Walker de Felix (1986) summarise work done in the United States in a model of acculturation which has four stages: 'tourist, survivor, immigrant and citizen', arguing that there is a significant difference between the first two and the second pair. This difference is characterised as an acculturation threshold of which they say (1986: 29):

> It is obvious that acculturation is to a significant degree but one manifestation of a general human response to new learning situations and growth, a reflection of mind as well as culture. It is not so obvious, however, exactly what this means for second language pedagogy.

This expression of uncertainty is an indication of the current state of debate among foreign language experts. On the other hand there is a substantial literature on the psychological representation of culture, on cultural contact and on the acquisition of cultural meanings.

In a summary of work on the psychological effects of inter-group, cross-cultural contact, Bochner (1982: 16) concludes that

> contrary to popular belief, inter-group contact does not necessarily reduce inter-group tension, prejudice, hostility and discriminatory behaviour. Yet one often hears politicians, church leaders and other public figures saying that if only people of diverse cultural backgrounds could be brought into contact with each other, they would

surely develop a mutual appreciation of their points of view and grow to understand, respect and like one another.

To this list of public figures might be added educationists in general and even language teachers in particular, although many of the latter have seen for themselves how, as Bochner says, 'at times, inter-group contact may increase tension, hostility and suspicion'. Attitude change does not follow automatically from mere exposure to another culture, whether in the form of direct experience or of the vicarious experience of the foreign language classroom. Bochner suggests that attitude change of a non-trivial kind 'involves a re-ordering of the individuals' cognitive structures, making them in a very real sense different persons' (1982: 23).

If we take the work in cross-cultural psychology seriously with respect to foreign language teaching, it is evident that English pupils learning French, for example, need to undergo some genuine cognitive process of change if the intention that language teaching shall create tolerance and, preferably, empathic understanding is to be realised. Merely exposing them to facts about France or taking them to the country for direct experience will not necessarily lead to desired educational outcomes and indeed may be quite counter-productive. Many teachers have noticed this, and pupils' own accounts are often remarkably frank about it, but what to do about it is not immediately obvious. Nonetheless Bochner's view does suggest that it is important to investigate how pupils' cognitive structures might change through language and cultural learning, and, consequently, how teachers might create the right circumstances for desirable changes to take place. It is thus to the work on acquisition of culturally influenced cognitive structures that we turn next. There is, however, no direct path into an account of how exposure to a foreign culture might influence cognitive structures—and hence attitudes—and it is necessary to begin with work on 'mother culture' and mother tongue acquisition.

Theories of language acquisition are much better known to language teachers than are theories of how the individual acquires the 'mother culture'. In foreign language (FL) theory, L1 acquisition theory is often 'extended' to L2 or FL theory. The nature of the 'extension' has varied from assumptions that L2 and L1 acquisitions are identical, to assumptions that there is 'interference' from L1 to L2 creating a need for an L2 theory which explains the negative influence of interference, to theories which attempt to explain L2 acquisition as a process of development of a new language system gradually separating out from the old, established language system (cf. Ellis, 1985; Littlewood, 1984). Because of the close and complex relationship of language and culture, it seems reasonable to make at least an initial approach following the pattern set in language acquisition theory and consider, first, what C1 acquisition consists of and what the relationship with C2 or FC might be. In his study of cross-cultural contact Bochner (1982: 28) also favours the analogy with second language learning.

One analytical approach, arising immediately out of the phrase 'acquisition of culture', is to isolate the two concepts and to ask 'what is culture?' and 'how is it acquired?'. In other words, 'culture' is perceived as an object and 'acquisition' a process focused on the object. A second approach consistent with the account of culture in Chapter 5 is to avoid separation of the two concepts, to view the process of acquisition as the dominant issue which will then lead on to a clarification or definition of culture. Furthermore, 'culture' is not considered to be an 'object' independent of subjects, of persons, of the process of subjects' acquisition. As suggested in Chapter 5, cultural meanings may have 'objective' reality in the sense that they are shared between subjects, but not in the sense that they exist independently of subjects.

Geertz (1975) considers the process of acquisition in phylogenetic and ontogenetic terms. His argument is that man developed biologically and culturally simultaneously rather than, as is one view, developing biologically a brain which could then 'invent' culture, which in this view is defined as a set of tools for mastering the natural environment. Geertz begins by defining 'mind' as 'a certain set of dispositions of an organism' developed in man in interaction with cultural and natural phenomena. His account of that development is worth quoting at length (1975: 82–3):

> The prevailing view that the mental dispositions of man are genetically prior to culture and that his actual capabilities represent the amplification or extension of these pre-existent dispositions by cultural means is incorrect. The apparent fact that the final stages of the biological evolution of man occurred after the initial stages of the growth of culture implies that 'basic', 'pure', or 'unconditional', human nature, in the sense of the innate constitution of man, is so functionally incomplete as to be unworkable. Tools, hunting, family organisation, and, later, art, religion and 'science' moulded man somatically; and they are, therefore, necessary not merely to his survival but to his existential realization.

Geertz's argument is based on evidence of phylogenetic development but is then extended to ontogenesis. Midgley (1980: 286) makes the same point succinctly and introduces the concept of instinct; 'man is innately programmed in such a way that he needs a culture to complete him. Culture is not an alternative or replacement for instinct, but its outgrowth and supplement'. Instinct is the nearest we can get to man's 'basic' nature, but it is not accessible in any 'pure' form. The individual's general cultural potential is realised by exposure to a particular culture—a parallel and integral development to the particular linguistic realisation of the individual's potential for acquiring a language. This means that the particular culture and its language will stamp the individual indelibly, will be an inseparable element of the individual's nature. Geertz supports this point with cross-cultural evidence. He suggests that the limitations of a particular culture and its language produce limitations in conceptual development. The structure of Arapesh language makes counting, which is based on a binary system, so difficult that the Arapesh are severely limited in mathematical development; their confinement to a binary system causes their lack of mathematical facility, rather than being a result of it (Geertz, 1975: 60–1). This kind of Whorfian claim is common in cognitive anthropology (Quinn, 1985; D'Andrade, 1985). Such observations could lead to speculation as to the effects on the individual of being exposed to two languages and cultures, particularly two which are fundamentally distant and distinct from each other; in other words, of having the linguistic and cultural potential realised simultaneously in two ways rather than one. The argument that bilinguals are psychologically different from monolinguals (Lambert, 1977) may be significant here. The evidence comes from the study of products rather than the process of a child's cultural development, but it is supported by work in neurolinguistics (Obler, 1983). The study of bicultural development may, however, be best conducted as a separate enterprise, rather than treating bilinguals as if they were a combination of two monolinguals, implying that monolingualism is the norm when statistically speaking it is probably the exception.

The study of the ontogenetic process of culture acquisition is treated by Vygotsky. Wertsch & Stone (1985: 164) quote what they call Vygotsky's 'general genetic law of cultural development':

> Any function in the child's cultural development appears twice, or on two planes. First it appears on the social plane, and then on the psychological plane. First it appears between people as an interpsychological category, and then within the child as an intrapsychological category. This is equally true with regard to voluntary attention, logical memory, the formation of concepts, and the development of volition.

Thus the child's potential is ontogenetically realised in interaction with others and much of that interaction is linguistic. It is in using linguistic—and other—signs that the child acquires meanings, and gradually recognises the meanings of signs which he has already used in social interaction without full cognisance of their significance. 'External' culture, in the sense of meanings and patterns of behaviour, is 'internalised' because of the individual's innate disposition to fulfil an incomplete potential. The child's disposition to acculturation is realised in a particular environment in interaction with particular individuals. This is not to say that what is internalised is some kind of mirror-image of what is present in the external environment, a simple agglomeration of experiences:

> The transformation of an interpersonal process into an intrapersonal one is the result of a long series of development events. The process being transformed continues to exist and to change as an external form of activity for a long time before definitely turning inward. ... The transfer [of functions] inwards is lined with changes in the laws governing their activity; they are incorporated into a new system with its own laws.
> (Vygotsky, 1971: 57)

The process of internalisation includes the acquisition of concepts, and thus the influence of a particular language and its meanings is crucial: 'Instead of viewing the meaning system of a language as mapping onto pre-existing cognitive processes, it is viewed as a social formation that plays a much more active role in the creation of consciousness' (Wertsch & Stone, 1985: 171). The role of adults is crucial too, for they structure the environment in such a way that a 'zone of proximal development' is created, which offers the child experience which is, as it were, one step ahead of its current state of development. They do this largely through language interaction with the child. Language and other semiotic systems are thus the carriers of culture, or, as Geertz (1975: 5) would have it, they *are* culture:

> The concept of culture I espouse ... is essentially a semiotic one. Believing, with Max Weber, that man is an animal suspended in webs of significance he himself has spun, I take culture to be those webs, and the analysis of it to be therefore not an experimental science in search of law but an interpretive one in search of meaning.

Geertz develops the notion of analysis in the following way (1975: 9):

> Analysis is sorting out the structures of significance—what Ryle called established codes, a somewhat misleading expression, for it makes the enterprise sound too much like that of a cipher clerk when it is much more like that of a literary critic—and determining their social ground and import.

He goes on to describe an event involving three 'frames of interpretation',

Jewish, Berber and French, and consequent misunderstandings. The level of generality of such a 'frame of interpretation' is not incompatible with the notion of established codes, routines, schemata or scripts, as more particular units of analysis have been variously called (Cole, 1985; Holland, 1985). Some of these units have been identified, according to Cole, by psychologists and others by anthropologists. Following Cole's attempt to combine work in psychology and anthropology, we can say that children internalise schemata of human knowledge from recurrent events in a particular sociocultural context. The sociocultural context can be described as the 'social space', the niche within which the child lives at a given point in time. It comprises essentially the people with whom he comes into contact—immediate or mediated—and the environment in which he lives: 'the society in its ecological setting seen from the individual's point of view' (Fortes, 1970: 27). Within that setting occur the recurrent events from which the child internalises schemata of knowledge. As the child grows, its social space expands and with it its knowledge. The advantage of linking the concept of social space with that of knowledge schemata is that a link can be made from the analysis of the psychological process of acculturation to the analysis of cultural meanings as they are embodied in the adult world, in their 'finished' shape.

Before considering the nature of that link, however, let us examine what might be meant by the notion of the child internalising schemata of knowledge. Rumelhart defines a schema as 'a data structure for representing the generic concepts in memory ... a schema contains, as part of its specification, the network of interrelations that is believed to normally hold among the constituents of the concept in question'. He points out that all kinds of concepts are included, 'those underlying objects, situations, events, sequences of events, actions and sequences of actions' (Rumelhart, 1980: 34). In discussing schemata and learning, he identifies three modes of learning: accretion, tuning and restructuring. Accretion is the most common kind of learning, when traces of experience, information processed by schemata, are laid down in memory. Tuning involves the modification of an existing schema to bring it more into line with a particular experience or number of similar experiences. This can lead to 'concept generalisation' when a particular modification makes the schema susceptible of handling a greater number of cases. The third mode of learning is the creation of new schemata, first by 'patterned generation' and second by 'schema induction'. 'Patterned generation' involves copying and modifying an established schema, learning by analogy. The distinction between this and 'tuning' is not clarified by Rumelhart but seems to be a matter of degrees of modification, until a modified schema is recognisably different from the original and the individual recognises that both the old and the new schemata are viable and useful. The notion of schema induction is described as follows (Rumelhart, 1980: 54):

> The notion here is that if a certain spatio-temporal configuration of schemata is repeated, there is reason to assume that the particular configuration forms a meaningful concept and a schema can be formed that consists of just that configuration.

Rumelhart points out that this notion of 'contiguity learning' is not a real necessity in a schema theory since, if a sufficiently general set of schemata is posited, then all learning can be accounted for in terms of tuning and patterned generation. Yet if the acquisition of concepts by young children is considered, then an explanation based on patterned generation from or tuning of a general set of schemata would have to assume an innate existence of that set of schemata as the child's 'starting point'. This would be contrary to Geertz's and Vygotsky's discussions of the ontogenesis and phylogenesis of cultural concepts unless the level of generality of the schemata were so high—approximating some notion of innate learning potential—as to be no longer compatible with the definition of a schema. Certainly, Geertz's definition of mind in terms of 'dispositions' would accommodate a highly abstract set of schemata, but the characteristics of a schema as defined by Rumelhart would be lost as a result and the explanation of learning in terms of patterned generation and tuning no longer tenable. Schema induction presupposes the existence of 'some aspect of the system sensitive to the recurrence of configurations of schemata that do not, at the time they occur, match any existing schemata' (1980: 54) which Rumelhart finds problematic for a schema-based system. In developmental terms, however, it fits well with the notion of a potential which is realised through exposure to the recurrent configurations of a particular culture.

This then takes us back to a Vygotskian perspective. Although Rumelhart does not discuss the role of language in schema theory, in so far as a schema is a means of representing a concept and 'corresponds to the meaning of that concept' (1980: 34) and in so far as language embodies meanings there is a complex of close relationships between schemata and language. The Vygotskian emphasis on language as a means of creating consciousness in the young child is compatible with schema theory but must imply that schema are created in the child as a result of social interaction, as a first stage, and are subsequently modified, tuned and serve as a basis for restructuring under the influence of new experience. The psychological process of acculturation can thus be linked to the analysis of cultural meanings in the adult world through the notion of schemata, and some schemata can be captured in linguistic analysis. D'Andrade exemplifies this in analysis of cultural models of individuals' character types, by analysing the terms used in American English to describe people, on the assumption 'that one important way in which people learn complex cultural schemata is through language' (1985: 321). By analysing the content and organisation of the semantic features found in sets of interrelated terms it is possible to discuss cultural models learned by all competent speakers of the language.

The analysis of the concepts of a specific culture is simultaneously an analysis of the schemata with which individuals order their experience. An analysis of the modifications which an individual makes as his 'social space' extends is an analysis of his acculturation to the different dimensions of the whole culture to which he is gradually exposed. Schema analysis would lead to an account of concepts and their interrelationships which are the meanings of a particular culture. This essentially static picture can be supplemented with the more dynamic notion of 'script' to account for individuals' socially-influenced actions.

The definition of scripts offered by Schank & Abelson (1977: 38), is that it is a standard event sequence. They are concerned with Artificial Intelligence and with creating mechanisms to recognise such scripts. Scripts are aspects of 'specific knowledge' which is used to 'interpret and partici-pate in events we have been through many times'. The coincidence with one aspect of schemata built up from recurrent events and internalised in childhood is evident, but Schank and Abelson are concerned with events rather than the wide range of concepts which schemata represent. Within their particular range of concern they distinguish specific knowledge from 'general knowledge' which 'enables a person to understand and interpret another person's actions simply because the other person is a human being with certain standard needs who lives in a world which has certain standard methods of getting those needs fulfilled' (1977: 37). This kind of knowledge they aim to encompass in the notions of 'plans' and 'goals'. To understand recurrent events the script is used; we recognise an event as being a realisation of a particular script. To understand situations we have never encountered before we use plans and goals; 'a plan is made up of general information about how actors achieve goals' (1977: 70). If by 'a world which has certain standard methods of getting needs fulfilled', Schank & Abelson refer to one particular society, then the level of abstraction from particular events, embodied in the 'plan', is not unlike the 'frame of reference' used by Geertz.

Schank & Abelson's main concern is with intra-individual data and they limit their claims to 'the world of psychological and physical events occupying the mental life of ordinary individuals, which can be understood and expressed in ordinary language' (1977: 4). They do not consider the notion of shared knowledge existing between individuals. Within these limits they suggest that 'whatever can be done with plans can be done in a more straightforward manner using scripts' (1977: 97). They do point out, nonetheless, that processing information based on plans is quite different from script-based processing. The amount of taken-for-granted knowledge in the latter, whenever a script is readily recognised, is much higher and more easily formulated than in plans. There remains a gap between knowledge which is acquired through recurrent routines and 'fixed' as scripts, and knowledge which underlies and is more general than particular scripts, and yet is peculiar to a particular sociocultural environment. Although the process of acquisition of such general knowledge is unclear—unless, for instance, it is envisaged as a distillation from a number of scripts—and although the taken-for-granted aspect of general knowledge is less readily accessible to the individuals, they formulate such knowledge nonetheless and use the 'frame of reference' to interpret what other people do and say.

Another theory, that of social representations (Farr & Moscovici, 1984) suggests that there are two fundamental processes by which we cope with new experience: 'anchoring', which 'draws something foreign and disturbing that intrigues us into our particular system of categories and compares it to the paradigm of a category which we think to be suitable' (1984: 29); and 'objectifying' which 'saturates the idea of unfamiliarity with reality' (1984: 38). It will be evident that Moscovici shares with Rumelhart the view that new experience is assimilated to and may in turn modify existing concepts. To what extent these processes differ in children and adults remains unclear, but these various notions of schema, script and social representation all point in the same direction and offer a reasonable basis for discussing the nature of exposure to experience of a foreign culture.

Let us consider the argument so far. We have an outline account of the relationship between a culture and the individuals living within it. The culture, understood as structured, interconnected webs or networks of meanings—largely but not exclusively embodied and manifest in linguistic formulations—triggers and shapes the development of the individual's 'mind', understood as dispositions, beliefs, skills, knowledge. Thus 'social' meanings, that is knowledge and beliefs, and 'social' skills and dispositions, are internalised under the guidance of older people and undergo such change that they become schemata of human knowledge by means of which individuals interpret and classify their experience of the world, including people and their actions. Schemata represent generic concepts, including those underlying sequences of events, which have been separately studied and defined as 'scripts'. The nature of the adult guidance offered is that the child is led through successive, ordered stages—'zones of proximal development'—by people in its environment. The people and the environment are significant in that their specificity determines to which social meanings the child is exposed and by which it is shaped as it grows. The analysis and formulation of the schemata by an outsider—whether at the level of heavily context-determined scripts or at increasingly context-free levels—is an interpretive skill not unlike the reconstruction and interpretation of a written text, which describes in a series of propositional statements the cultural meanings of a given society or sub-section of it.

Let us now attempt to relate this account of the acquisition of culture to cultural studies, first by discussing the 'cultural baggage', as it is sometimes called, which pupils bring with them to the foreign language classroom, and, second, by asking what we can hope to do once they are there.

It will be evident from the foregoing account that the pupils who enter the classroom do not in fact carry 'cultural baggage' which they can set down and leave outside the door. The metaphor is misleading. The pupils are rather an embodiment of the culture which they share with others. Without them, and others, culture would not exist, and without culture they would not be recognisable as human beings. This general argument applies to language in particular, which is the most important means by which culture is acquired and shared with others. When externalised and shared, much of culture can be described by formulating it in language, by interconnected statements of the meanings. It can also be externalised by other means, such as painting or music. Indeed, many societies contain individuals who spend much time attempting to externalise the accessible and sometimes almost inaccessible meanings of culture—we call them artists. Their work externalises meanings in ways which often need further exegesis—the work of the critic—but in ways which embody the complex interconnections as criticism cannot.

The pupil has internalised culture, which becomes part of his whole being, over a period of years, in fact since birth. He has been 'taught' culture in a series of steps. The step-like nature of the process is to be understood in two ways. First, he has gone through a series of stages, which have been carefully structured by others. Second, his exposure to 'others' has been gradual, as the 'social space' in which he exists has expanded and he has acquired new and modified schemata of knowledge. He has moved from home and family through increasing numbers of friends and friendship institutions, teachers and schools, from experience which is direct to that which is mediated by others, by books, by television and other media. He is a creation of his environment although he is unique in his viewpoint and experience of the environment. In so far as he shares and re-externalises and reconstructs the meanings of his environment, he negotiates, and constantly renegotiates, the meanings of his culture, and his schemata of cultural knowledge are modified. Some of the meanings and their schemata representations are the ones which give him and his group its particular sense of belonging together as a group, that is those meanings which create a sense of community (Taylor, 1971) and those which mark the boundaries of the community (Barth, 1969). The group may be ethnically, socially or politically determined, and he will usually belong to more than one group. In so far as negotiation of these particular meanings is limited to a particular network of people, it is different from his negotiations within other networks to which he may belong. In overlapping networks, however, there are overlapping negotiations and agreements on meanings, which are not crucial and particular to the identity of the group, and thus there are overlapping cultures. Where there is no overlap, there is no shared culture. For the individual in this case, this means his schemata do not coincide with those of an individual from another culture. However, in the Western world under the heavy influence of mass communication and as a result of historical development, there are some cross-cultural, shared meanings even at an international level. The need, however, to mark group identity and cohesion at various societal levels still produces breaks in communication, and community-creating meanings not shared outside the group.

The pupil who enters the English classroom to learn French belongs to and is in part shaped by a national culture which has some overlaps with the culture of a French pupil in French society. He has a national identity—as well as other identities—which excludes him from knowledge of the meanings which underlie French national identity, and which is sustained by those meanings and schemata which mark his English culture. Let us consider, first, how the teacher might expect the pupil to develop psychologically. Consider the case of French teaching begun in an English secondary school at age 11, as the pupil enters secondary school. The transfer to secondary school is a perceptible stage in the extension of the pupil's social space. The experience involves exposure to a wider range of teachers, of adults offering guidance in the pupil's acquisition of new schemata of knowledge. Some schemata are now markedly determined by traditions within academic disciplines of knowledge, but there are many others which are more informal, embodying the hidden curriculum of schooling. The subject 'French' takes its place among the competing claims on the pupil's attention. There is, however, a potentially significant difference.

In other subjects the pupil is exposed to new experience which is a development of existing experience, where existing schemata of knowledge are 'tuned' to bring them into line with new experience. He is also introduced to new areas of knowledge, as his social space expands, and he acquires new schemata through 'patterned generation'. The subject 'French' on the other hand both offers new experience and reconsiders old experience, much of which is part of primary and secondary socialisation. Berger & Luckmann (1971: 150) in their account of socialisation have a tantalising comment which they leave undeveloped:

> We may leave aside here the special question of the acquisition of knowledge about the objective world of societies other than the one of which we first became a member, and the process of internalizing such a world as reality—a process that exhibits, at least superficially, certain similarities with both primary and secondary socialization, yet is structurally identical with neither.

The issue they raise, however, is that learning French language and culture is a fundamentally different experience because it requires a reassessment of schemata which are basic to the development of the individual mind. The research is still tentative, but in neurolinguistics there is evidence of change within the brain of bilinguals which is produced by second language learning: 'learning a second language must necessarily change language organisation within the brain—if "only" at the cellular level, then pervasively nonetheless' (Obler, 1983: 164). This may apply to foreign language learning too, if the learning is effective. A simple example is the fact that pupils learn to tell the time again or learn the colours of the spectrum. More complex examples are the distinction of *tu/vous* and the social roles implied, or the definition of what is edible in one culture and the difference from definitions of what is edible in another. There is no denying the shock for English people of learning that French people eat snails, or for French people that the English eat turnips!

Consider how this new view of old experience might be encompassed within Rumelhart's account of schema theory. The possibilities are three: tuning, patterned generation or schema induction. Whichever possibility is realised there is no question of simply 'repeating' earlier schema formation in some kind of separate conceptual space. The determination of which possibility will be put into operation is conceivably influenced by two interconnected factors: the degree of difference of the new experience from existing schemata and the degree to which differences are made perceptible, largely by the teacher. Again there is some indication of what this may mean neurolinguistically in research on bilinguals: 'within the neurolinguistics of bilinguals, we assume that the different ways a second language is learned and used, not to mention differences in the actual language structure themselves, will participate in determining brain organisation for language' (Obler, 1983: 188). Take the example of colours. It is frequently the case that pupils equate '*rouge*' with 'red' and '*brun*' with 'brown', yet the arbitrary division of the spectrum in French culture differs from that in English culture, with the effect that a part of the spectrum called in French '*rouge*' is in English 'brown'. The simplest pupil response is to continue to use the English colours and assign new labels to them, thus misusing the French words, as if they were a codification of English words. A more complex response is to 'tune' the existing schema to encompass a wider definition of 'red', to include parts of 'brown'. This may, however, do such violence to the old schema that a new schema has to be created through patterned generation, by analogy. The case of *tu/vous*, however, cannot be dealt with by analogy, given the lack of a perceptibly comparable phenomenon in English. Again, violence can be done to the phenomenon and it can be assimilated to notions of 'you-singular' and 'you-plural'—which some teachers do as a first stage of explanation—but it is more reasonable to envisage the creation of a new schema by induction. The role of the teacher lies in the question of whether the pupil is encouraged to assimilate new experience to old schemata or whether, by careful structuring of the pupil's zone of proximal development, he encourages the pupil to develop new schemata. The new schemata would then represent an alternative to, rather than a replacement of, old schemata, and their operation would depend on context.

Let us take now the experience in French which is a development rather than repetition of previous experience. The first point is that this is more like the experience of other aspects of schooling, where the pupil's 'social space' is extended and through the help of others new concepts are introduced. Examples of this kind of learning are knowledge of French history and geography or French institutions, such as are frequently considered in 'background studies'. Where 'background' information is offered in the same way as, say, English history, the pupil is not required to tune or restructure existing schemata. Where information is presented from the perspective of the foreign culture, with deviation from the pupil's normal cultural expectancies, then there will arise the need for restructuring of schemata by patterned generation or schema induction. This points to the significance of the teacher's role, in the first instance, in creating the other cultural perspective on new experience. The teacher also, by tradition, presents the new experience in carefully measured and structured amounts.

There is, however, another way in which learners meet new cultural experience under the influence of a foreign perspective: by first-hand experience of the foreign country. Potentially this requires a massive re-organisation of learners' cognitive and affective structures, a large-scale modification and development of their schemata. The length of the stay and the degree of isolation from others from their own culture may be reasonably supposed to increase the pressure on learners to accept the foreign culture perspective. On the other hand they may find this pressure unbearable and suffer what is commonly called 'culture shock' (cf. Furnham & Bochner, 1986). Teachers who take pupils to France, particularly on exchange schemes, know this phenomenon well.

The study of people's reactions to residence in other cultures is not extensive. There are the first-hand, introspective accounts of researchers who have resided in other cultures for their own purposes, typically anthropologists reflecting on the rigours of fieldwork in exotic societies (e.g. Wax, 1971; Williams, 1967). There are empirical studies by social-psychologists who attempt to measure change in individuals' beliefs and behaviours. In his review of this latter research, Bochner (1982: 16) says that 'ethnic contact research cannot be said to have been conducted with a great deal of theoretical sophistication'. As we saw at the beginning of this chapter, his review of research into attitudes, social perceptions, attributions and behavioural indices leads him to put forward a theoretical model, with some supporting empirical evidence, which, in order to account for attitude change, postulates 'a re-ordering of the individuals' cognitive structures, making them in a very real sense different persons' (1982: 23). Bochner then identifies four types of outcome of residence abroad: passing, chauvinistic, marginal and mediating. The first three produce undesirable effects such as loss of ethnic identity, retreat into nationalism and identity confusion at a personal level and assimilation, intergroup friction and social change at a societal level.

The fourth involves 'personal growth' at the individual level and 'intergroup harmony, pluralistic societies and cultural preservation' at the societal level:

> There is evidence that some individuals can select, combine and synthesize the appropriate features of different social systems . . . such individuals [are called] mediating persons, people who have the ability to act as links between different cultural systems, bridging the gap by

introducing, translating, representing and reconciling the cultures to each other.
(Bochner, 1982: 29)

It is this which could be the best form of empathic understanding integral to the aims of foreign language teaching, although it is more likely to be attained by the university student than by the school pupil. The other three are a useful reminder that mere exposure to the foreign culture does not automatically lead to desirable outcomes, whether through residence abroad or through classroom language learning. Why some experience leads to desirable outcomes and other experience does not remains a matter for further research, but the implication of Bochner's model is that 'a desirable outcome may be achieved by creating or controlling the social climates of particular settings' (1982: 30). This would imply that the teacher's control over cultural learning is crucial, and that the place which teachers can most fully control, the classroom rather than the period of direct contact with the foreign culture, has a significant role to play in preparing learners so that their reaction to the direct contact will be a desirable one. What then should foreign language teachers be trying to do? What kind of cognitive and affective changes should they hope for and how should they render the environment and experience propitious for these changes?

We have argued that one of the aims of cultural studies teaching should be to produce changes of attitude in pupils towards other cultures and that attitude change is dependent upon change in cognitive structures. We have also argued that the cognitive structures which reflect cultural meanings, particularly those which are the base of community in a society, should be the focus of the teacher's efforts, in particular those meanings which mark the boundaries between one community and another. It is those cognitive structures or schemata which reflect boundary-marking common cultural meanings which cultural studies teaching should be attempting to change. In the first instance the schemata which embody individuals' sense of their own ethnic identity determine how they experience other cultures and other people's ethnicity, and it is these schemata which need to change if these individuals' perceptions of others are to change—and their attitudes towards them.

In order to bring about change in schemata—by patterned generation or by induction—individuals need to be brought into contact with new phenomena, to have new experiences. Yet simply to bring them into contact with foreign cultures and peoples will not be adequate, since they deal with this through their existing concepts of what is 'foreign', and it is not the reinforcement of these existing concepts which is the purpose. Of course, if they experience foreign phenomena which cannot be dealt with by existing schemata, then change in those schemata should take place, but in the foreign language classroom the vicarious nature of the experience will normally mean that existing schemata will cope adequately, and merely be reinforced. Because we suggest that schemata or concepts of what is foreign are linked with those of one's own ethnicity—through emphasis of contrast and difference—we can begin with pupils' schemata of their own ethnic identity in order to influence their schemata of what is foreign. To bring about change in pupils' schemata of their own ethnicity, we need to confront them with new experience of their ethnicity. This can be done by presenting them with a foreigner's view of their ethnicity, with the intention that their existing schemata of their own ethnicity shall change when they cannot cope with the new experience. Such new experience needs, of course, to be agreeable and non-threatening, so that pupils are prepared to change their schemata rather than reject the experience by assimilating it to their existing views of foreigners; they must be helped to take seriously foreign views of themselves which differ from their own, and to adjust their own to give recognition to the foreign views.

The next stage is to help them to reconsider their own views of foreigners, to change their schemata of foreign cultures and peoples in general and of the culture under study in particular. This might be approached through experience of the particular foreigner's view of his/her own ethnicity, that is of the boundary-marking meanings which he/she uses to maintain ethnic identity. In the English situation, this would mean that English pupils would, as a first stage, meet French views of English ethnicity and, at the second stage, experience French views of French ethnicity. In the course of this experience intended to change cognitive structures—that is, schemata of what it is to be English and what it is to be French—the teacher has the further responsibility of educating pupils in the discipline which underlies cultural studies: social anthropology. The teacher must not only present experience but also provide pupils with the concepts of the discipline which will help them cope consciously with the new experience.

I turn again to Hurman's book *As Others See Us* (1977) which gives some indication of how the presentation of others' views of English identity can be linked with anthropological concepts. Where she uses material from a wide range of sources, but all in English, the French teacher would present French views of the English in French. Hurman also attempts to move to the next stage, of considering English views of others, but this too would be focused on the French in the foreign language teaching situation. Hurman's material is a mixture of pictures and written text, mainly from the mass media, especially newspapers. The French teacher's material could be more diverse than this.

However, it is not easy to find French views of English ethnicity, partly because they are not conscious or articulated by French people; the same applies to other nationalities *mutatis mutandis*, including English views of the French. It is no less difficult to find French accounts of French ethnicity—at national, regional or any of the other levels which, we have argued, might be introduced at various stages of language learning—for the same reasons. The collection of material is therefore not straightforward. It is hampered by the lack of consciously articulated accounts, and with regard to material which gives an indirect account needing interpretation, the question of representativeness arises. How do we know that material collected from one person or group of people is representative for a whole group, whether a nation or a region or social class or whatever?

Taking the issue of representativeness first, it is one which is recognised by ethnographers. Since they do not select their informants by statistical sampling, how do they know that the few people they use are representative? This is not the point at which to review the literature debating this issue, but in brief one view is that individuals' acquired cultural competence is a version of society's shared culture, and that that version is systematically influenced by the social roles the individual plays (Boster, 1985). Thus any one individual's cultural competence is representative partly of the consciousness which all members of his society share and partly of the societal groups—residential, social class or other—to which he belongs. The individual's representativeness can therefore be accepted without the need for statistical sampling, but needs to be complemented by individuals from other societal groups.

If, however, we are primarily interested in that part of the individual's competence which represents the meanings shared by all the members of his society, irrespective of sub-group membership—and this is what we mean by boundary-marking phenomena at a national level—then most individuals and particularly adults can be assumed to represent their society. The problem of articulation of this unconscious competence still remains. How are we to tap the unconscious schemata which embody the common meanings of ethnic identity and views of others' ethnic identity? How are we to obtain articulate accounts of French ethnicity from a Frenchman and articulate accounts of the French view of English ethnicity?

One technique which might lend itself to solving this problem is Kelly's repertory grid method of collecting individuals' constructs (Bannister & Maier, 1968). For example, French people just arrived in England—one group is that of the students who come as French Language Assistants—are likely to be particularly aware of their own and English ethnicity in the early stages of their sojourn. They might be interviewed in depth about their experience, using both informal interview techniques and the repertory grid method. The interviews might in themselves provide teaching material in the foreign language. In addition the researcher might interpret the text of the interview, guided by frequently used consensus constructs collected through the repertory grid, and begin to establish a consensus account, a culturally shared view of what it is to be English and French. This would then serve as the basis for determining the selection of more indirect accounts of ethnic identity, in the form of teaching materials which embody and illustrate, in the first stage, French experience of English ethnicity, of some English cultural meanings and, in the second stage, French experience of the cultural meanings which embody French ethnicity.[1]

Conclusion

Like other chapters in this book, this one can have no simple conclusion. The chapter has explored some of the psychological theories which might help foreign language teachers and researchers better understand how what they are trying to do might be realised in practice. As long as they are interested, such theories can serve heuristically to guide teachers' practice. In the longer term the theories must be put to the test, modified or rejected. Language teaching practices will in the meantime continue to develop and will themselves help researchers to refine their thinking. The benefits of theory and practice can and should be mutual. Empirical research helps to forge the link. It is to empirical research that we turn in the next chapter.

Note to Chapter 6

1. The pilot research project referred to in the preface is beginning to explore just these ideas at the moment of writing.

7 Cultural Knowledge and Cultural Information— Some Empirical Evidence[1]

We shall begin the argument of this chapter by positing a distinction between cultural 'knowledge' and cultural 'information', which will be related to the account of psychological processes outlined in Chapter 6 and the account of culture as experience in Chapter 5. The chapter will then go on to discuss some empirical research, including textbook analysis, and interviews and observations of teachers and pupils.

By 'knowledge', we refer to the presentation of ideas, concepts, facts and material about or from the foreign country and people in a structured way. Thus 'knowledge' is 'structured information', and more than the aggregate of facts contained within its structure. The nature of the structure may vary according to pedagogic and other principles discussed below, whereas information involves the arbitrary and decontextualised presentation of facts with only minimal and usually unprincipled structure.

Let us take a simple example of the kind which is frequently seen in the teaching of French. Learners are often told about food in France and French eating habits; the fundamental importance of the topic in all cultures is perhaps reinforced by stereotypes of 'French cuisine'. *Information* about *'le déjeuner'* would include the following:

— that this meal is eaten at midday
— that the break from school and work lasts up to two hours
— that it is a substantial meal of hot dishes with several courses, with examples given
— that the whole family will sit down to this meal together.

On the other hand, *knowledge* of this aspect of food and eating habits would have at least the following dimensions:

— an explanation of the relationship of the midday meal to the general pattern of meals throughout the day, e.g. that *le petit déjeuner* is a light meal perhaps taken at different times by members of the family as they leave for school or work; that children have *le goûter* at about 4 o'clock so that they are able to wait for the *souper* or *dîner* at 7 or 8 o'clock in the evening

— an explanation of patterns of work and schooling, e.g. that school and work start early and finish late in the afternoon so that a substantial break and meal in the middle of the day is welcome and that the similarity between times of starting and finishing school and work creates the opportunity for the whole family to eat at the same times at midday and in the evening.

The presentation of *le déjeuner* as information by a teacher or a textbook might involve the general pedagogical principles of developing the presentation from the simple to the complex and relating the information to learners' existing knowledge. Without modification and development, however, this approach will lead to the isolation of simple facts and comparison with an apparently similar phenomenon in English food and eating habits, or rather to the version of them known to the particular group of learners be it 'lunch' or 'dinner'. Such a presentation is a tacit invitation to learners to assimilate the information to an existing schema of meal-time patterns and eating habits. As suggested in Chapter 6, assimilation to existing schemata may be problematic if the new phenomena are too unlike the familiar realisations, but the distance created by vicarious presentation in the classroom probably allows assimilation to take place on the grounds that *'le déjeuner'* is 'really' just a, literally, outlandish version of the normal and natural midday meal as it is known to the learners. At best, some 'tuning' of the existing schema may take place but this will depend on the degree to which the teacher emphasises the difference, for example by stressing the differences in the content of the meal.

In Chapter 5, it was argued that a native view of cultural experience different from that of an outsider is necessary for the culture to be understood in its own terms. Further, the ideal of empathic experience of the foreign culture requires learners to be exposed to aspects of the culture in the complexity which propositional description and interpretation can facilitate but not simulate. Information about French meals and eating habits would provide neither a native view nor the opportunity for complex experience. It is also part of the argument of Chapter 5 that direct experience need not lead to understanding, that without explanation and interpretation such experience can be treated as information and assimilated to existing knowledge schemata. The oft-repeated claim in the interviews discussed below that 'it's just the same as here really' came equally from those with and without direct experience of a foreign culture.

Consider now the structured presentation of knowledge of French meals and eating habits. In Chapter 6, it was argued that the *tu/vous* distinction when presented in its full cultural context cannot be assimilated but must result in the creation of new schemata by what Rumelhart calls induction or contiguity learning. An interpretation of meals and eating habits which included the explanations suggested above would similarly necessitate the creation of new schemata especially if accompanied by direct experience, for it would break the mould of the existing schemata by obliging learners to take the French cultural schema as a mode of understanding the facts described. They would no longer be 'outlandish'.

It was to investigate to what extent current practice takes account of issues such as these that an empirical study was carried out over three years in two comprehensive schools in the north of England.[2] The research cannot be discussed here in detail and it is the intention simply to cite some relevant aspects. In particular we shall consider what kind of information or knowledge was offered to pupils and what they and their teachers thought of it.

Analysis of a Textbook

It quickly became apparent from classroom observations that the content and direction of lessons, and in particular their cultural content, were strongly influenced by the textbook made available to the teachers. The textbook in question is *Action! Graded French* which consists of five volumes published in the early 1980s (Buckby, 1980). The writer's declared aim is to equip learners with sufficient French to cope with short visits to the country. This has, however, to be viewed critically and an evaluation made not simply in terms of whether the book fulfils the declared aims. In fact, this approach is likely to lead immediately to a presentation of information rather than knowledge because the notion of surviving and coping suggests that the learner remains within his own framework in dealing with the alien environment. Let us consider then how French culture is presented in the first three volumes of the series, i.e. the books read by the majority of pupils who then opt out of French and all other kinds of language learning in the English secondary school.

The textbook is specifically intended for the teaching of French language, in a classroom context, to 11- to 16-year-olds. In addition, the author states they are intended 'to develop an understanding of, and to foster positive attitudes towards, countries where French is spoken and to speakers of French' (Buckby, 1980: 3).

Action! embodies the 'communicative approach' to language teaching and as such emphasises the learning of the language for clearly defined purposes, and these are outlined in the general objectives for the textbook. The communicative approach, together with Buckby's commitment to fostering positive attitudes towards the French, has very definite implications for the image of France portrayed. Buckby hopes to equip children with the necessary knowledge to be able to visit France with a school or his/her family. This knowledge consists of language and skills for coping with situations likely to arise during a visit, and ranging from finding a place to stay to coping with a breakdown in the car. Such situations can be seen in his selection of geographic location, characters and situations.

The presentation of information in *Action!* takes several forms:

— black and white photographs of people, places or items from France
— simple sketches, drawings and cartoons varying from small cartoons to maps and drawings of items for exercises
— English or French (in volume 3) text presented as factual, or as talk by characters in the book. This can cover several pages or a few lines and includes geographical and historical information, and information about customs and habits. It also ranges from personal descriptions by characters used in the textbook to more general accounts.

Each volume is divided into a number of units, each addressing a different aspect of French life. The way in which an author organises the textbook into chapters and the content of each chapter illustrates his or her priorities, what he or she sees as the important subject areas to cover. The *Action!* volumes are divided into situations in which a pupil could find him or herself on a visit, such as ordering a meal, asking the way, or introducing him or herself to a family. This is particularly clear in the units devoted to French food, of which there are 11—the greatest number on any one theme. The first mention of Food is in Book 1, where there are six units devoted to buying or ordering and paying for food in either a cafe or a shop. The range of foods is at this stage quite limited, in keeping with the cafe situation. In Book 2 the range of foods is widened and the situations are in the home. In Book 3 food is covered in a restaurant in keeping with the setting of Book 3 in Paris.

Thus the situation and general content of *Action!* dictate the content of more specific cultural information. Books 1 and 2 vary from Book 3 not only in that the location changes from Boulogne to Paris but also in its more generalised presentation. Whereas in Books 1 and 2, two children give a personal, though very brief, insight into French lifestyle, in Book 3 the commentary is on the whole anonymous and detached, much more the outsider's view.

Analysis by theme is the most appropriate means of analysis of the text since the approach in *Action!* is a thematic and problem-oriented one. Throughout the books specific problems of a visit to France are addressed under specific themes, ranging from asking directions to finding a place to stay and booking in. Each problem is addressed by providing the relevant vocabulary and phrases and brief information about the situation in general and what might arise.

Let us take one such theme, that of using public services, especially transport. Since the emphasis in the volumes in question is upon enabling students to visit France, a large proportion of each text is devoted to using services which include transport and other communications; this also includes shopping, although most of the shopping described relates to food. There are separate units devoted to travelling by bus, coach and train, sending a telegram and using the post office. Also in Book 3, there are three units concerned with driving in France. This type of description accounts for nearly a quarter of all the units in *Action!* Books 1–3. Information consists of maps and diagrams, signposts and photographs of the means of transport or communication, of tickets and of people undertaking, or about to undertake, journeys or phone calls and so on. *Action!* describes the processes of undertaking a journey, phone call or whatever in detail, from knowing where to go and what to do, to asking for information. It is in this area that the strictly functional nature of the information is most obvious.

As intended by the author, the first three volumes of *Action!* do present a positive image of France as a country and of the French people. The emphasis is at all times upon being able to enjoy a visit to France and communicate with French people in this country or abroad.

The country is presented positively mainly through locating the textbooks in Boulogne and Paris, real places that children may visit, or have heard of, where there is apparently lots to do and see. This place-of-interest view of France is portrayed through descriptions, pictures and characters' accounts. It is supported by the text's concentration upon leisure activities, travel and eating out and is strongest in the third textbook set in Paris. The positive view of the French people is most strongly portrayed through the pictures of people. Throughout all three books they are all smiling, attractive people, and on the whole young. People offer help and directions generously, and particularly in Book 1 there is a great deal of handshaking and greeting. Any negative aspects of the image are due to the inevitable dating of photographs. A book which relies heavily upon photographs for a dynamic and contemporary approach quickly becomes out of date.

The overall impression *Action!* gives on France and the French people can be compared with a royal visit, since it seems a fair assumption that only a royal visit would run so smoothly without glimpsing less attractive or more mundane features of French life. French driving is the only subject dealt with in a critical way where one of the characters states:

> While I've been finding my way around Boulogne I've been amazed at the speed of the traffic ... There are crossings marked on the roads with white lines, but don't expect the cars to stop for you if you want to stay alive! (Book 1, p. 33)

At the end of Book 3 there are two units, one about breaking down in France, the other about a car accident, which are a departure from the generally flawless approach to France. Two other images stand out from the rest of the textbook for a similar reason. A rabies advert takes up a whole page of one volume and there is the repeated image of the policeman with revolver, although it is stated policemen are generally helpful.

Generally the view of France and French people is not stereotypical. The people are presented as being very similar to people in England and the volume of pictures of 'ordinary'-looking characters outweighs the occasional stereotype, such as Coco the frog hand puppet and those to be found in the cartoons.

On the author's own criteria, then, the books are satisfactory. His criteria stem from his implicit view of cultural knowledge as a crutch for 'practical communication' when learners are in France. It is apparently assumed that this image will also 'foster positive attitudes', although the link between 'positive image' and 'positive attitudes' remains unproven.

An evaluation can only be in relation to the standpoint taken towards the aims of cultural studies in foreign language teaching. Risager & Andersen (1978) offer criteria in terms of realism. 'Realism' in this sense is not principally a question of accuracy and comprehensiveness in the depiction of life in France. It refers, rather, to the degree to which the reader may perceive and accept the image presented—no matter how partial—to be real. Behind Risager & Andersen's criteria lies a philosophy of promoting cultural knowledge not simply for utilitarian or attitudinal purposes but also to encompass socialisation through foreign language learning, the philosophy defended in earlier chapters of this book. In a literary sense 'realism' can be defined in terms of readers' perceptions and their dependence on the portrayal of real places, situations and people which are believable because they are similar to what we already know. According to the criteria stressed by Risager & Andersen, for an accurate view of another culture positive and negative aspects are important and it is clear that *Action!* emphasises a positive France and neglects negative features. Risager & Andersen argue that for cultural studies to be realistic, the universe must be,

a. balanced, comprehensive
b. at micro and macro level
c. positive and negative.

The immediate problem this raises is that no account is value-free and objective. The view that the textbook gives of France and the extent to which this appears to be real is rather an issue of presentation of a perspective or section of life which is recognisable as real. For example, the characters must be credible, the places and the institutions must be possible. This approach to realism is one applied to the novel by Hough (1966: 114) when he states,

> We should be wrong however to judge a novel by the amount of social and historical reality it incorporates. It is not a quantitative matter. The novelist is perfectly free to make his own selection from the available social and historical material, and it may be a narrow one. We do not ask in reading Jane Austen 'But where are the lower classes?' or if we do we are foolish. Jane Austen tells the truth about a certain segment of the middle class of her time, from the viewpoint of a woman who herself belongs to that class.

Thus *Action!* can be analysed for what it is, a selective description of France and French people, within which the issue of providing some balance between positive and negative aspects is still important. The image of France and the nature of the information given usefully fulfil the more instrumental of Buckby's objectives: to equip a child to visit France for a holiday or short exchange visit (including a description of how to show French pupils around his/her own school). However, these objectives are not necessarily compatible with the more general educational aim of promoting understanding of French people and developing pupils' social awareness. This can be seen quite clearly in *Action!* where the image of French people is superficial and so positive that it is hardly believable; we do not get close enough to understand them and there is virtually no basis for empathy such as possible shared problems and attitudes. The superficial portrayal of the people leads to a less realistic image.

On the other hand, *Action!* does provide a realistic view of two French towns: Paris and Boulogne. The geography is real, the places exist. Photographs of places and items reinforce this. The choice highlights the issue of places having to be *perceived* as real which is at least as important as their actual existence. Paris and Boulogne are probably the two places children are most likely to have heard of and to visit (and of course this can now work in the opposite direction with teachers choosing places to visit that the children are studying). On the other hand, it is highly debatable whether Paris and Boulogne can be said to represent France as a whole. Thus as far as topographical realism is concerned, the use of photographs of actual places and people lends credibility, even though the selection may be unrepresentative, lacking in comprehensiveness.

In summary, the view of France and its people is consistent with a functional 'communicative' approach to language and cultural studies. In its limited way the places and situations appear to be realistic. The development of characters remains limited, which makes them appear less real and the issue of understanding them is not dealt with in any depth. Although the view of France and its people is a very attractive one, the selective image of *Action!* Books 1 to 3 lacks:

— the less attractive realities of everyday life which would make the image more credible and thus perhaps create greater empathy for the people
— a more sensitive and probing approach to French people and French lifestyle
— a description and consideration of some of France's institutions, for example its politics and religion.

One of the implications of the image is that although France is presented positively, it contributes very little towards an understanding of the French.

Observation of teachers using *Action!* and discussions with them indicate that the information-oriented character of the books is complemented by teachers' views and classroom techniques. It is difficult to know to what extent teachers are influenced by the books or the books written under the influence of teachers' views, but the harmony between the two is striking.

Interviews with Teachers

Although a clear distinction must be maintained between what teachers say and what they do in class under the pressures of the situation, it is useful to consider how teachers in the research saw the purpose of cultural studies teaching.

There are common views expressed by teachers concerning the role and importance of cultural studies in language teaching. These can be divided roughly into two areas: those which relate to the development of children, and those confined to the aims of the lesson. When asked if and why cultural learning is important the teachers generally talked about how it is important for children to know about other ways of living which may or may not be better than their own. Through such knowledge they may become more tolerant of other peoples and less restricted in their own lifestyle. One teacher says:

> You have got to be adding something to the kids' lives other than the ability to say 'Je suis Anglais' . . . They have got to be able to say at the end of it, yes well I have learnt this and that or that about French people or about France so that you have actually changed their concepts, especially around here . . .

Another says:

> . . . I always tell them straightaway that there is more to life than Newfarm because they honestly can't see more, and that one way out is to travel and see what other possibilities there are, and that they will improve as people if they can see how other people are and they needn't be wasting their time say not knowing what to do in Newfarm. This helps me of course because I say—have a language, do something with it and off you go. Obviously plugging my subject. But I feel the quality of life differences should be stressed because children like them miss out and don't realise it.

So there is a general philosophy among these teachers of positively developing personalities. In addition, cultural information is seen as a pedagogic device for capturing the interest of pupils, contextualising their language learning, giving light relief or filling in lessons where language learning is believed to be limited. This second function is briefly expressed in the second quotation above. Other teachers talk about how important it is for the country to be made real to the learner rather than 'a nondescript place' or 'never never land'.

These all link with ideas some of the teachers have about children's ethnocentricity being exacerbated by their particular geographical location, in the north of England. A third teacher says:

> Children are very quick to say that is stupid, but you have got to try to explain to them that a French person may find what we do stupid and it is just a difference and not necessarily an inferiority.

And a fourth puts the point as follows:

> I think the difficulty is they can't see a purpose in French living here in Hillside. I have got to give them an example of a situation where it is going to have a use.

The first teacher quoted says:

> . . . there is such an ingrained intolerance of foreigners in this area. . . . I am sure teaching French to kids in Kent with day trips to Calais or Boulogne must be a totally different experience. I mean some of them if they want to can go to Dover and look at the damn place. You know for these kids it could be a million miles away. I think that is the greatest difficulty we face and it's something we can't do anything about because it's a geographical fixture.

It is thought by the teachers that including cultural information in French lessons is necessary and important for the management of their lessons and as a way of improving their pupils' general education and development. How then do pupils themselves think about the teaching of French and cultural studies in particular? The research offers some insight into this from interviews with approximately 100 pupils, lasting on average approximately 45 minutes.

Interviews with Pupils

The research was focused on pupils in the third year of secondary schooling. Among many other things it was possible to talk to them in semi-structured interviews about their perceptions of the teachers and the textbooks. For example, the following quotation comes from a pupil taught by a teacher who was observed to introduce a lot of her own experience into discussion of French culture, usually in anecdotal form:

> **Pupil**:   She tells us everything that she can about it.
> **Interviewer**: That's the sort of—just the little things from everyday life
>   or what?

> P: Just the little things from everyday life really—to tell you more about the people.
>
> I: More than there is in the textbook perhaps?
>
> P: I can understand her more than the textbook—because she describes people well enough—and in the textbook they seem to be more like us really—but like when you go over there they seem to be different—I can understand her more than the textbook.

Another pupil gives an insight into the methods he finds interesting:

> And she brings us—teacher brings us a lot of like things to show us—and maps and other things—so we can understand—she doesn't like just say that's a stamp there and show it round the class holding it in her hand—she passes it round so we can have a look and that—and she explains everything.

In the course of the interviews a number of pupils commented upon the cultural studies aspect of French lessons. From questions posed upon possible improvements to textbooks it was apparent that some pupils would prefer to have more cultural information included:

> I: Do you do more language than about France?
>
> P: We do about France and then it mingles with about France when we learn about the language, the vocabulary and that.
>
> I: Which do you prefer?
>
> P: ... Learning about it better, 'cause I'd like to find more about the place, rather than how to say where's the toilet and things like that I'd rather learn about the place.

This view was shared by another pupil from the same school:

> I: What would you put in?
>
> P: Well, just personalities and that. What they are like. We never do nothing about what they are like.
>
> I: Can you explain that a bit more then? That is the sort of thing I am interested in.
>
> P: We never do what kind of things they do on a night, go to youth clubs or anything like that. Never do anything about that.
>
> I: Right, so put that kind of thing into the textbook. You are thinking of people of your age now?
>
> P: Yes.
>
> I: What about older people. Would that be of interest to you?
>
> P: Yes.
>
> I: What would you want to put in about older people?
>
> P: What they do. What they do for a living, things like that.

The amount of cultural information was thought to vary according to the year of the course:

I: Have you enjoyed your French so far?
P: Yes.
I: Equally all the way through?
P: Yes, it's more this year 'cause it's not all—in the first two years it was all language but this year we're doing a bit like French—the way of life in France.
I: And that's more enjoyable?
P: Yes.

Conversely, for a number of pupils the first two years of the course were recalled as providing more cultural information and were thus recollected more favourably than the third year:

P: It's pretty boring, we just do the same words over and over again. Just sitting there—it goes in one ear and out the next.
I: Have you always thought in the same way about French?
P: No, before I used to enjoy it. First and second year I used to really enjoy it. When you like learned different things all the time. Now we just do the same things. Doing like weather—can't think what we are doing now.
I: Well, when you say you do different things what do you mean?
P: Like we were going off, now we're doing food, like before we did our family and like pets. Then the history, things like that that we did. Then we did the weather, now we are doing food, weights of food, what you eat like for dinners, teas. Dragging it all out.

Where distinctions were drawn between linguistic and cultural aspects of French lessons the latter were usually positively evaluated. Pupils in the higher achievement groups did not differ from those in the lower achievement groups in their appraisal of this aspect:

Well, the language and verbs are a bit dry, you don't like doing that, but when you're learning about what French people do, like how they speak and things like that I enjoy it.

It could be argued that while the majority of those of both high and low achievement appreciated the cultural studies component, it was enjoyment of the linguistic aspects which was more likely to differ between the higher and lower sets. For some in the lower sets learning about France provided a welcome respite from the acquisition of linguistic skills:

I: What are the bits that you like most then?
P: Just talking about different places in France.

I: What is it you don't like about it or that your mates don't like about it?

P: ... When we are talking to the teacher because we are frightened we might get wrong.

I: You find it difficult then sometimes?

P: Yes.

Some of those who were not going to continue taking French after the third year did retain positive views of the cultural studies aspect:

I: What did you enjoy about it?

P: Learning about French people, what their habits were, what they eat.

There were, of course, some cases in which the linguistic aspect was preferred:

I: Do you like learning about the country at all or are you not particularly interested in that?

P: No, not particularly interested.

I: I was just going to say do you prefer that or do you prefer learning the language?

P: Languages 'cause they're quite fun, 'cause we just learn everyday things but ...

Occasionally neither aspect was found of interest:

P: Just don't like it. Too hard.

I: It's too hard. The language?

P: Yes.

I: Would you like to learn something about France without the language? If you didn't have the language problem?

P: No.

As a comparison group, similar interviews were conducted with junior pupils, i.e. before they began to learn French. It was found that no junior pupils referred spontaneously to the cultural studies aspect of French lessons. For most the image of French lessons was confined to the acquisition of linguistic skills. Older siblings were an obvious source of information about French lessons as well as about the language itself. However, those aspects of French lessons thought to be most interesting by secondary school pupils, such as learning about France and taking an active role by engaging in dialogue, had not been understood by the younger age group to form part of the content of future lessons. It was possible that their conception of likely secondary school lessons was bounded by notions of more passive written work:

> Just like reading out of books and things, out of French phrase books or something like that and getting the pads and drawing a picture or something like that.

Some were aware of other aspects of learning French from hearing older siblings:

P: ... My brother learns it at school and I like the language.
I: Have you heard some?
P: Yes, 'cause when he comes home he always—he used to tape some of his voices and I used to go and listen to the tape and I like that.
I: Listen to him on the tape?
P: Yes, he used to—they used to do homework on tape, they used to have to speak what they'd learnt. I liked that.

She continued later:

P: Er ... he likes them [French lessons], he says it's not really hard because the letters are helping you all the time you're learning it and ... once you've started it and you start learning more about the country instead of just the language, more about the country itself, and that's why I'm looking forward to going there next year. 'Cause we're going to know more about it when we go up to the secondary school so I'm looking forward to that.
I: What exactly would you like to know about the country?
P: About the people and about how they live, what their houses are like and things like that and ... shops and how much things are compared to what they are in Britain, things like that, that will help us when I go to the next school.

Some negative aspects of lessons had been unfortunately transmitted:

P: ... My brother said at school that they just race through a tape fast and you have to get it right, I'm not looking forward to that bit.

With prompting, the occasional pupil realised that speaking French formed part of the content of lessons, but even if the following individual eventually realised this the predominant image is of 'book work':

P: Mainly language and my brother has this notebook about words written down in French and he tells us to test him and I say the French word and he says the meaning. So I am really interested in the meaning of the words, the French words.

> **I:** So what do you imagine you will do in the lesson then? What kind of exercises, what kind of work will you do?
>
> **P:** I reckon like it will be like you get down, you sit down and you get your books out. It is not mainly writing I don't think. It is reading I think because if you can read a language you can write it. Whereas if you can write it you might not be able to read it.
>
> **I:** What about speaking?
>
> **P:** Speaking? Yes that's it. That's what I mean. Getting to speak fluently.

It was only when pupils were asked directly if they were looking forward to learning about France that the cultural studies aspect was mentioned. When discussing whether they were looking forward to learning French they referred spontaneously only to their concern with acquiring linguistic skills:

> **P:** Well words like that.
>
> **I:** Would you like to learn about the people and the country?
>
> **P:** No, I would just like to learn about words.
>
> **I:** The language?
>
> **P:** Yes.

When prompted upon this aspect pupils were unsure whether they would find cultural studies of interest.

> **I:** OK. Would you like to learn anything about France?
>
> **P:** Yes, I'd like to learn a bit about it, the sort of things they do, what different ways and that.
>
> **I:** And you're looking forward to learning French?
>
> **P:** Yes, in a way.
>
> **I:** In a way, why in a way, you're not too keen really?
>
> **P:** I'm not sure, I'd like to learn about it but I might not like it, learning about other countries and that.

For one pupil the reason for learning about a country appeared to be linked to touristic reasons:

> **I:** Would you like to learn about the country and the people?
>
> **P:** Yes. Like the attitude of them. If they were like fussy, fussy and like learn how they live and what kind of food they eat and you would know more if you wanted to go there or not.

Conclusion

The last pupil cited is not without ambition to experience other countries, peoples and ways of life. Yet he clearly feels insecure and concerned about whether he would find France congenial to his normal lifestyle. His tendency to see France as the sort of place where one might spend a holiday is one which teachers and textbook writers are tempted to seize on as the basis for their work. There is, however, a fundamental difference between catering for this touristic curiosity and developing the pupil's social understanding of another culture. The teachers quoted above are aware of this but the textbook they use—and the practices it encourages, which have not been described here—is not destined to help them develop pupils' ethnocentric curiosity into an empathy with other culture and a different people.

The investigation of practice and the effects on pupils' understanding and attitudes is an issue to which the extracts above cannot do justice. Only a full account of the research could do that. Nonetheless, this chapter points to the need for a review of practice and proposals for change. The final chapter is a step in that direction.

Notes to Chapter 7

1. This chapter is written jointly by Veronica Esarte-Sarries, Susan Taylor and Michael Byram.
2. The study in question is a research project funded by the Economic and Social Research Council, entitled 'The effect of language teaching on young people's perceptions of other cultures'.

8 A Model for Language and Culture Teaching

The purpose of this chapter is to develop a theoretical model which embraces the philosophy of language and culture teaching expounded in earlier chapters and incorporates the insights acquired from considering sociological, anthropological and psychological theories. The implementation of a model developed from theory will doubtless be more problematic than an approach based on the modification and development of existing practices. Nonetheless, a theoretical model may be less tainted by existing prejudices and can serve as a yardstick against which to measure development and change in existing practices. The procedure adopted here will be to present the model briefly and succinctly as a whole and then to discuss aspects of it separately and in more detail. This second stage will also deal with questions of implementation.

The Model

I have already argued that culture teaching needs to draw on the disciplines of the social sciences, especially cultural and social anthropology, in order to determine what shall be taught and why. Similarly, culture teaching needs to have regard to work in social psychology in order to understand and foster the psychological processes which learners may be expected to experience in the course of exposure to a different culture. Thirdly, the peculiar relationship between language and other aspects of culture—and the traditions of language teaching itself—require particular consideration. Thus from a social anthropological point of view it is possible to consider teaching culture through the learners' own language, for from this point of view this language is used in a specific way to interpret the other culture (Agar, 1985). From a psychological and linguistic viewpoint, however, it is necessary to create modifications in learners' concepts and schemata by a process of further socialisation and experiential learning in the foreign language, which itself embodies the foreign culture. Since, however, the acquisition of the foreign language at secondary school inevitably lags behind the maturation and socialisation process, the use of the learners' first language has to be invoked to some extent in the modification of existing and still developing perceptions of culture and society.

There are, therefore, two possible approaches: first, the use of learners' first language as the medium of study of a foreign culture, taught according to the principles of appropriate disciplines, although without the intention of introducing the learner to the totality of the culture. Second, the integration of language and culture learning by using the language as a medium for the continuing socialisation of pupils is a process which is not intended to imitate and replicate the socialisation of native-speaker peers but rather to develop pupils' cultural competence from its existing stage, by changing it into an intercultural competence. In schema-theoretical terms, this involves a modification and change of existing schemata to accommodate new experience. It is in sharp contrast with the practice of providing pupils with a consumer-tourist competence which offers them the opportunity to reach a critical threshold, enabling them to survive in the foreign and, by implication, hostile environment of the foreign country. What is at issue here is a modification of monocultural awareness. From being ethnocentric and orientated simply towards boundary-marking phenomena, as seen from their existing viewpoint, learners are to acquire an intercultural awareness which recognises the function of boundary-markers and the existence of other centres of ethnic identity with different perspectives on both boundary-marking and unmarked phenomena.

One consequence of this approach is to introduce into the foreign language classroom learning which is similar to that in other subjects. In particular this kind of teaching involves pupils in using language—in this case both first and foreign languages—as a tool for learning. The long debate and considerable research (Stubbs, 1983) devoted to the role of language, both written and spoken, in pupils' learning consequently becomes relevant to the foreign language teacher in ways not apparent hitherto. For the first time, the phrase 'Language Across the Curriculum' used in the Bullock report (D.E.S., 1975) and the work of researchers such as Barnes, Britton & Torbe (1986), Edwards & Furlong (1978) or Wells (1987) become central to the concerns of the foreign language teacher, and there is need for empirical research in this tradition applied to foreign language teaching.

In practice the two possibilities ought to be combined. The use of the learners' mother tongue for comparative analysis of own and foreign cultural meanings can be combined with the teaching of the foreign language as a subject and as the medium of experience of foreign cultural phenomena. This would involve, first, language learning in the current sense of skill-acquisition, enriched by the study of the nature of language as a social and cultural phenomenon (Language Awareness). Second, the study of language would in turn be combined with a study of culture, both of these carried out with comparative techniques using the learners' mother tongue. Thirdly, the direct experience of selected aspects of the foreign culture from the viewpoint and within the ethnic identity of the foreign peer group would be in the foreign language, and this would in turn contribute to the language learning process. The whole process can be represented as a circle of techniques and experience (see Figure 1).

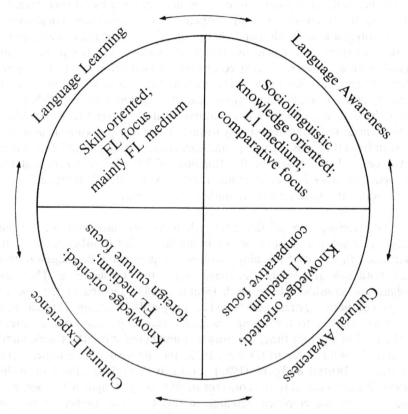

FIGURE 1. *A model of foreign language education*

The mutual support of each quarter of the circle with the two adjacent quarters is represented by the double-headed arrows. Cultural Awareness develops out of and parallel with awareness of the sociolinguistic dimension of language study by comparative analysis of, for example, the semantic fields of the two languages, and their relationship to cultural meanings. Cultural Awareness is also mutually supportive with the direct experience in the foreign language of selected cultural phenomena by allowing for L1-medium analysis of that experience and of the relationship between the language and cultural meanings of the experience. Language Awareness will also have beneficial effects on the acquisition of linguistic skills by allowing learners to reflect on their learning, but in turn will be supported by the experience of learning if the language learned is made the focus of comparative analysis. Finally, the relationship between Language Learning and Cultural Experience is mutually supportive in that Language Learning may well be largely rehearsal-oriented with some communicative teaching techniques shifting the learner towards performance—e.g. by information gap exercises—and this shift can be made more realistic by using the language as a medium and for experiencing and talking about cultural phenomena presented from the viewpoint of native-speaker peers and adults.

So far the four sectors of the circle have been represented as being of equal size, implying the same amount of time devoted to each. The amount will, however, be determined by the stage of learners' development and the emphasis and time allocated to any one sector will vary as pupils advance. This point will be considered again in the detailed discussion of the various aspects of the model.

Language Learning

The advances in language teaching made under the banner of Communicative Language Teaching are welcome because they have switched emphasis to active use of the language as a technique for learning and acquisition, and have taken some note of the social character of language embodied in the notion of a speech act. Furthermore, Communicative Language Teaching has stressed the use of 'authentic' language as the material from which pupils learn, providing them with experience of language produced by native speakers, even though in the initial stages it may have to be carefully selected if it is to remain accessible. The conception of language competence in terms of know-how or skills which have only a tenuous relationship with knowledge about the language in question has led to a re-emphasis of language use as a form of language learning. Provided these various shifts in emphasis do not become exclusive of, for example, the ego-centred use of language in imagination and thought or the conscious manipulation of language which does undoubtedly benefit from knowledge about its structures, whether rhetorical or grammatical, the Communicative Approach provides pupils with a satisfactory process of language learning, and there is no need to add to the considerable literature on its refinements and developments. The Communicative Approach provides pupils with immediate experience of the language both in those activities which emphasise rehearsal and practice of skills and in those which, by dramatising language use in role-play and simulations, introduce learners to language as social action. Nonetheless, despite 'authentic materials' imported into the foreign language classroom, the experience is a restricted and limited version of using the language in the foreign culture and society, and the principal focus remains on the language and on learners' fluency and accuracy in language use.

Language Awareness

The development of language awareness teaching (Donmall, 1985; Hawkins, 1987) has stressed both the need to educate children in one of the fundamental characteristics of being human and, secondly, the benefits in language learning of having a general understanding of the nature of language and positive and realistic attitudes towards language learning. The potential range of topics on which to construct a language awareness course is so large that selection has to be made both with a view to restricting the extent of a course and with regard to the learners' age and cognitive capacities. In general, courses have introduced pupils in the early secondary years to topics in the sociology and psychology of language, with some forays into philological and grammatical issues. Lessons on first language acquisition, on dialects and other language varieties, on historical and contemporary relationships between different languages or on social attitudes towards speech and writing can all contribute to the two principal purposes of educating about language and preparing the ground for language learning.

In the model proposed here it is in the analysis of sociological and structural aspects of language that the language awareness component will contribute most directly to the whole. For, by presenting learners with the opportunity to understand the relationship between language and other cultural phenomena, this component allows them to link their acquisition of language skills with their understanding of the foreign culture. In so far as the study of first language acquisition also includes the relationship between language acquisition and culture-specific socialisation, the psychology of language is also directly pertinent. Since selection is inevitable, one new criterion should be the contribution which a particular topic can make to this linking function between language learning and cultural awareness.

For example, in language learning pupils acquire the skills and some linguistic formulae needed to greet and take leave. These may be practised in role-play, and be acquired through experiential learning. The language awareness component would draw conscious attention to the similarities with and differences from the learners' first language, perhaps focusing on different degrees of formality and the appropriate linguistic formulae. Yet this issue of formality is inextricably linked with cultural knowledge of social structures. The linguistic formulae are the surface indicators of native speakers' cultural knowledge, which is itself largely unconscious and difficult to articulate. In order to help pupils to understand that cultural knowledge, the teacher would compare with their own inarticulated cultural competence and begin to make them aware of the nature of cultural behaviour in general as well as of how to act acceptably in the specific foreign culture in question. This would differ from much current practice which would keep the focus on fluent and accurate use of the language while providing simple recipe-like recommendations on when to put the linguistic formulae into operation. Cultural awareness teaching thus shares with language awareness a dual purpose of supporting language learning and extending general understanding of the nature of culture.

The proposal for a new selection criterion would probably mean a greater concentration in the language awareness component on the particular language of the language learning component. In many language awareness courses, the net is cast widely to include examples and illustrations from many languages. Although this has many advantages—not least the possibility of drawing on the languages spoken by bilingual pupils—the new criterion would mean a new focus in the available time and less opportunity for wide-ranging lessons. This would, however, be offset by a greater cohesion between the two components, overcoming some of the problems of current courses, and would introduce more opportunity for using and simultaneously analysing the particular language in ways not available within the communicative approach. The dominant teaching medium would remain the learners' mother tongue, as in current language awareness courses, as the demands of abstract discussion and the kind of learning which will change attitudes and schemata of concepts require use of learners' first language.

Cultural Awareness

The similarities in purpose between the language awareness and cultural awareness components have already been mentioned. Both are concerned with specific and general learning. Both are concerned with the relationship between language and culture. The cultural awareness component is also concerned with non-linguistic dimensions of culture and more focused on the question of change from monocultural to intercultural competence.

In his off-beat account of anthropological fieldwork Barley (1987: 58) recounts how an African chief offered him a drink of beer in a calabark and how, his own training notwithstanding, he foolishly imported a custom from his own culture:

> Possibly I was infected by his own courtliness. Whatever the reason, instead of simply draining the cup as would have been expected, I held it up and proclaimed Zuuldibo's name in a toast. Immediately a deep and shocked silence descended upon the gathering. The boys stopped talking. Zuuldibo's smile froze upon his face. The very flies seemed hushed from their buzzing. I knew, as everyone knows who works in an alien culture, that I had made a serious mistake.

To rectify the damage he is forced into a role-reversal, where Zuuldibo becomes the ethnographer and Barley himself 'the confused and hopeless informant'. For he finds it very difficult to explain the custom of toasting one's host and Zuuldibo is understandably doubtful about how saying someone's name can prolong a person's life and make them happier. Eventually Barley seizes on a concept he knows is familiar to Zuuldibo and says toasting is 'like the opposite of cursing', thus rescued after all by his ethnographer's training and his ability to make coherent comparisons which the layman might not be able to do.

> It was the famed 'comparative method' of anthropology in action, an enlightening example of a way in which we both had half a picture that was meaningless until put together. I was also discomfortingly aware of how Zuuldibo had forced my thought into paths that were not their own. Until I discussed it with him, I had no clear thoughts at all about toasting, about why we did it, what we expected its effects to be. It was very disconcerting.
> (Barley, 1987: 59)

It is the feeling of being disconcerted which is an indication of a change of attitudes and concepts, of a modification of schemata, which cultural awareness teaching should bring about. Barley's comparative method differs from practice in foreign language classrooms precisely because of the reversal of roles. Current practice is more akin to the attitude of the ethnographer who seeks to understand and explain the culture, although foreign language teachers and learners seldom go to the lengths of trying to understand the cultural phenomena they notice from the viewpoint of the other culture. Cultural awareness teaching should, however, involve both viewpoints, making learners both ethnographer and informant, allowing them to gain a perspective through comparison which is neither entirely one nor the other. In the process of comparison from two viewpoints there lies the possibility of attaining an archimedean leverage on both cultures, and thereby acquiring new schemata and an intercultural competence. Hurman (1977: 1), in her attempt to introduce anthropological knowledge and ethnographic methods into the school curriculum, has a similar formulation:

> I have had three aims in writing this book: first and most important, to help us to see how we, as odd and amusing or irritating foreigners, are seen by other peoples; second, to help us see how other peoples see themselves; third, by building on this double understanding, to be able to look at and understand ourselves more clearly than before.

Although foreign language teachers may bridle at the emphasis on the learners' own culture and selves, it should not be dismissed without more ado. For an intercultural competence and a deeper self-understanding are far from being mutually exclusive. The particular value of Hurman's book, however, is that it is practical, has been piloted in schools and demonstrates the Brunerian point that the most abstract of concepts can be made accessible to young people. Through newspaper articles, stories, pictures and illustrations from daily life, she introduces the notions of stereotype, category and role within our own society. She then expands the horizon to compare categories within different societies, taking her examples from kinship terms, a crucial area of anthropological study. She then deals with racial stereotyping and prejudice and moves on to problems which arise—not unlike Barley's—when two cultures meet. Hurman's work has an affinity with Bruner's 'Man: a Course of Study' in its generality and concern with using specific illustrations from a range of cultures in order to support some abstract concepts concerning the nature of self, of otherness, of man as a species, which have been developed within social science.

Foreign language teaching, on the other hand, is traditionally concerned with only one language and culture and the teaching of general concepts would normally be seen as incidental. Even were this to change in favour of teaching more than one language and culture, during the normal five-year course, it is unlikely, although nonetheless desirable, that the scope will be extended beyond the languages spoken in the developed world—possibly including the new immigrant languages from the Third World. Moreover, the emphasis on the link of language and culture and experience of the foreign culture in and through the language means that Hurman's explicit framework of social science concepts illustrated by whatever ethnographic material seems appropriate—from British newspapers to Evans-Pritchard's studies of the Nuer—would have to be reversed, with the emphasis on introducing pupils to one specific, usually Western European, culture and the use of social science concepts as a means to that end. However, since Western European cultures are in themselves complex and multi-layered, there is still opportunity for selecting material from a wide range of sources. The advantages Hurman gains from being able to select from markedly different cultures is that the fundamental contrasts are very clear, whereas comparisons across European cultures can very easily stop at the level of superficial customs and habits whose significance as symptoms of underlying beliefs is not explored. It is assumed that beneath the surface all Europeans have essentially the same culture and 'civilisation'.

To summarise, the cultural awareness component would examine the phenomena of, say, French culture and by so doing would have a number of purposes. It would provide a further opportunity for comparative study of French and the learners' mother tongue by examining the use of French in French culture, for example by concentrating on key concepts and their linguistic manifestations. It would cause learners to reflect on and explicate their own key cultural concepts, however disconcerting this may be, thereby making them see themselves as others do and modifying their existing schemata and cultural competence. The content of this component would be in part drawn from the language learning and language awareness components and in part dependent on the cultural experience component of the model. For the cultural experience component would of necessity give little opportunity for reflection, both because the emphasis would be on immediacy and directness of experiential learning and because, taking place in the foreign language, learners would need the chance to stand back from the experience and reflect upon it in their first language.

Cultural Experience

The fourth component of the model serves as a bridge between study of the culture and learning of the language, but it is not simply an opportunity to apply or put into practice the abstract cultural study and the rehearsal of linguistic skills. For this fourth component introduces another kind of learning, through direct experience, of the relationship between language and culture, of the way in which language is part of culture and also embodies the whole.

Cultural experience is widely available already to pupils in secondary schools, through exchange holidays, educational visits, contact with native-speaker teachers and assistants, family holidays and so on. In the best cases, links with language learning are made incidentally and deliberately, for example by giving pupils tasks to carry out 'for real' which they have many times practised in role-play and simulation. The emphasis on linguistic survival in a foreign environment which such exercises may imply, however, is inimical to the link with cultural awareness which is also desirable.

If this link is to be made, direct experience of the foreign culture needs to be structured in such a way that it gives learners insight into the culture from the native speaker's viewpoint. It is not the intention or hope that, by some undefined process of immersion, learners will become native speakers culturally any more than linguistically; they shall not change identity and abandon their own cultural viewpoint. It is rather a question of suspension of disbelief and judgement for a period of experiential learning, which is prepared for in the cultural awareness component and later analysed there too. Learners need to be prepared for experience of the daily rhythm of the foreign culture, of the behaviours which are different and those which are the same but have a different significance. Such phenomena are verbal and non-verbal, and learners need both the skills of fluency and accuracy in the language and the awareness of the cultural significance of their utterances. Direct experience of the foreign culture is therefore not the culmination of language and culture learning, not the final performance for which all else is rehearsal, but rather an integral contribution to the whole process which is prior to, simultaneous with, and subsequent to other components.

Furthermore, not all cultural experience need take place in the foreign country. That aspect of a stay abroad which consists of using the foreign language to cope with new experience by modifying existing schemata, can also be found in the classroom when pupils are taught through the foreign language. This is most evident and best known in Canadian immersion programmes but is also apparent in 'sections bilingues' or 'internationaux' where pupils are taught part of their normal curriculum in the foreign language. When pupils are introduced to new concepts in geography or new foods in home economics lessons in the foreign language, their new experience is embodied in the language.

Were this kind of teaching to take as its subject matter the particular culture associated with the language used as a medium, then the learning involved would be similar to that in the stay in the foreign country. It would not be as complex and rich, but learning to cook the food in a home economics lesson focused on the specific culture would be comparable with cooking and eating the food in the foreign country. Similarly, being introduced to new concepts in geography through study of the particular country in the foreign language would involve a non-mediated learning of the foreign viewpoint, provided the geography were taught as it is in the country itself. As with cultural experience in the foreign country, this kind would need preparation and subsequent analysis in both language learning and cultural awareness components. It would, however, also serve as a bridge between these two by providing opportunity to turn language rehearsal into performance and by creating experience on which to reflect in more abstract terms in the mother tongue. This notion, which might be called a 'section biculturelle', would be different in scope and purpose from existing 'sections bilingues', but the success of the latter, where they exist, is an indication of the feasibility of this aspect of the cultural experience component.[1]

Balance and cohesion of the four components

It was stated earlier that the four components are mutually supportive and integral to the whole and that the balance and proportion allocated to each will vary within the period of learning. It will also be evident from the preceding discussion that the components are not separate entities to be taught exclusively of each other. It is particularly the case that language and cultural awareness overlap in content and teaching method, and there is a different kind of mutual dependence between language learning and the 'section biculturelle' dimension of cultural experience. The change of emphasis and allocation of time to each component will to some extent occur in detail from week to week within a course. However, it is possible to establish theoretical guidelines as to appropriate emphases over larger periods of time.

In order to make the discussion more concrete, let us consider a five-year course of secondary school foreign language learning. This is about the usual minimal length in European countries and, with approximately three hours per week, offers some 120 hours of teaching time per year. In the first year, approximately 60% of the time should be spent on language learning, 20% on language awareness and 10% each on cultural awareness and cultural experience. In this first year pupils are keen to make swift progress in the foreign language and this can be supplemented by language awareness work which draws extensively on the particular language they are learning, dealing largely with sociological and psychological dimensions.

In the second year the language learning component can be reduced (50%) to benefit cultural experience (20%) and the first moves towards '*section biculturelle*' teaching. Similarly, language awareness and cultural awareness can be given equal proportions (15%), although with more emphasis on structural and semantic issues in language awareness there will be increased overlap between the two. This pattern can be held through the third year too, although the '*section biculturelle*' proportion of cultural experience may increase from year to year.

In years 4 and 5, there will be a decrease in language learning and a marked increase in cultural experience, particularly through *section biculturelle* work, since the practical difficulties of providing long periods in the foreign country will in most cases preclude what might be theoretically desirable. Thus by the end of the fifth year, in the optimum case, language learning will be reduced to about 20%, cultural experience increased to 40% and language and cultural awareness components will be allocated 40%, divided approximately equally. To summarise:

Year	L.L.%	L.A.%	C.A.%	C.E.%
1	60	20	10	10
2	50	15	15	20
3	50	15	15	20
4	20	20	20	40
5	20	20	20	40

(approximately 120 hours per year over 5 years)

This kind of allocation would be anathema to many language teachers who consider that any time spent on work other than language learning must be minimal. Yet it is a potential realisation of the philosophy of language teaching defended in earlier chapters. That philosophy has to be represented in practical terms and the methodological theory developed from the social and human sciences also needs sufficient time to be put into practice. In other words, such an allocation is a clear way of recognising the general educational value of language learning as well as its vocational and instrumental applications.

Note to Chapter 8

1. I am grateful to the staff of Goff's School, Hertfordshire for allowing me to visit and discuss with them their *'section bilingue'*.

References

ACTON, W.R. & WALKER DE FELIX, J., 1986, Acculturation and mind. In J.M. VALDES (ed.), *Culture Bound*. Cambridge: C.U.P.

AGAR, M., 1985, *Speaking of Ethnography*. Beverly Hills: Sage.

ALLARDT, E., 1979, *Implications of the Ethnic Revival in Modern, Industrialized Society*. Helsinki: Societas Scientiarum Fennica.

ALPTEKIN, C. & ALPTEKIN, M., 1984, The question of culture: EFL teaching in non English speaking countries. *ELT Journal* 38, 1, 14–20.

ANDERSEN, H.G. & RISAGER, K., 1979, Fremmedsprogsundervisningens socialiserende funktion. *Forskning i Fremmedsprogspaedagogik*, Copenhagen: Statens humanistiske Forskningsråd.

——1981, 'What did you learn in French today?' *ITL* (Louvain) 53, 23–36.

ANDRÉ, M. 1983, Use of content analysis in educational evaluation: doing prose analysis, *Discourse* 4, 1, 1–12.

APLIN, T.R.W. *et al.*, 1981, *Introduction to Language*. London: Hodder and Stoughton.

APU (Assessment of Performance Unit), 1985, *Foreign Language Performance in Schools*. London: Department of Education and Science.

BANNISTER, D. & MAIER, J.M.M., 1968, *The Evaluation of Personal Constructs*. London: Academic Press.

BARLEY, N., 1987, *Plague of Caterpillars*. Harmondsworth: Penguin.

BARNES, D., BRITTON, J. & TORBE, M., 1986, *Language, the Learner and the School* (3rd ed.). Harmondsworth: Penguin.

BARTH, F. 1969, Introduction. In F. BARTH (ed.), *Ethnic Groups and Boundaries*. London: Allen and Unwin.

BAUMGRATZ, G. 1982, Die Funktion der Landeskunde im Französisch-unterricht. *Praxis des neusprachlichen Unterrichts* 29, 2, 178–83.

BAUMGRATZ, G. & NEUMANN, W., 1980, Der Stellenwert des Vergleichs im landeskundlichorientierten Fremdsprachenunterricht. *Jahrbuch Deutsch als Fremdsprache*, 6, 161–80.

BENEDICT, R., 1961, *Patterns of Culture*. London: Routledge & Kegan Paul.

150   CULTURAL STUDIES IN FOREIGN LANGUAGE EDUCATION

BERGER, P.L. & LUCKMANN, T., 1971, *The Social Construction of Reality*. Harmondsworth: Penguin.

BOCHNER, S. (ed.), 1982, *Cultures in Contact*. Oxford: Pergamon.

BOSTER, J.S., 1985, 'Requiem for the omniscient informer'; there's life in the old girl yet. In J.W.D. DOUGHERTY (ed.), *Directives in Cognitive Anthropology*. Urbana: University of Illinois Press.

BRISLIN, R.W. *et al.* (eds), 1971, *Cross Cultural Perspectives on Learning*. New York: John Wiley.

BROWN, H.D., 1980, *Principles of Language Learning and Teaching*. New York: Prentice Hall.

BRUMFIT, C., 1984, *Communicative Methodology in Language Teaching*. Cambridge: C.U.P.

BRUNER, J.S., 1966, *Toward a Theory of Instruction*. Cambridge, Mass: Harvard University Press.

BUCKBY, M., 1980, *Action! Graded French*. London: Nelson.

BURSTALL, C., 1974, *Primary French in the Balance*. Windsor: NFER.

BUTTJES, D. 1981, Fremde Lebenserfahrungen im Englischunterricht. Landeskundliches Lernen mit Texten der oral History, *Sprache und Beruf*, 2, 29–39.

——1982, Landeskunde im Fremdsprachenunterricht. *Neusprachliche Mitteilungen* 35, 1, 3–16.

——1983, Texte für den landeskundlichen Fremdsprachenunterricht. In A. RAASCH *et al.* (eds), *Beiträge zur Landeskunde im Fremdsprachenunterricht*. Frankfurt a.M.: Diesterweg.

BUTTJES, D. & KANE, L., 1978, Theorie und Zielsetzung der Landeskunde im Fremdsprachenstudium. *Anglistik und Englischunterricht* 4, Mai, 51–61.

BUTTJES, D. & SUCK, P., 1977, Kommunikationssituationen in Lehrwerken für den Englischunterricht. *Linguistische Berichte* 51, 67–78.

BYRAM, M.S., 1979, Performance objectives and language learning. *Modern Languages* 60, 2, 111–15.

——1981, Language teaching within a framework. *Curriculum* 2, 2, 11–14.

——1982, Where is the 16+ leading us? *British Journal of Language Teaching* 20, 3, 145–48.

——1983, Are modern languages useful? Are foreign languages useful? In F. COFFIELD & R. GOODINGS (eds), *Sacred Cows in Education: essays in reassessment*. Edinburgh: Edinburgh University Press.

——1984, Cultural Studies in Language Teaching. *Modern Languages* lxv, 4, 204–12.

BYRAM, M.S. & SCHILDER, H., 1986, As Others See Us. *Praxis des neusprachlichen Unterrichts* 2/86, 2, 167–73.

CHARTE DES LANGUES VIVANTES, LA, 1980, *Les Langues Modernes* 1980, 309–19.

CHURCHILL, S., 1986, *The Education of Linguistic and Cultural Minorities in the OECD Countries*. Clevedon, Avon: Multilingual Matters.

COHEN, A.P., 1982, Belonging: the experience of culture. In A.P. COHEN (ed.), *Belonging—Identity and Social Organisation in British Rural Cultures*. Manchester: Manchester University Press.

COLE, M., 1985, The zone of proximal development: where culture and cognition create each other. In J.V. WERTSCH (ed.), *Culture, Communication and Cognition*. Cambridge: C.U.P.

COOKE, M., 1973, Social psychology and foreign language teaching. *Foreign Language Annals* 7, 215–23.

D'ANDRADE, R.G., 1984, Cultural meaning systems. In R.A. SHWEDER & R.A. LEVINE (eds), *Culture Theory*. Cambridge: C.U.P.

——1985, Character terms and cultural models. In J.W.D. DOUGHERTY (ed.), *Directions in Cognitive Anthropology*. Urbana: University of Illinois Press.

D'ANGELAN, A. & TUCKER, G.R., 1973, Communicating across cultures. *Journal of Cross-Cultural Psychology* 4, 121–30.

D.E.S., 1975, *A Language for Life*. London: H.M.S.O.

——1981, *The School Curriculum*. London: H.M.S.O.

——1984, *Foreign Languages in the School Curriculum—A Consultative Document*. London: H.M.S.O.

——1986, *Foreign Languages in the School Curriculum—a Draft Statement of Policy*. London: H.M.S.O.

D.E.S. and Welsh Office, 1985, *General Certificate of Education: the National Criteria—French*. London: H.M.S.O.

DEUTSCHER, I., 1968, Asking questions cross-culturally: some problems of linguistic comparability. In H.S. BECKER (ed.), *Institutions and the Person*. Chicago: Aldine.

DEUTSCHMANN, A. 1982, Grundlegende Aspekte der Landeskundeplanung, *Praxis des neusprachlichen Unterrichts*, 29, 2, 123–32.

DODSON, C.J., 1967, *Language Teaching and the Bilingual Method*. London: Pitman.

DONMALL, B.G. (ed.), 1985, *Language Awareness*. London: C.I.L.T.

DOUGLAS, J.D. (ed.), 1970, *Understanding Everyday Life*. Chicago: Aldine.

DRESSLER, G., REUTER, B. & REUTER, E., 1980, Welche Landeskunde braucht der FU? *Linguistik und Didaktik* 43/44, 233–51.

DUIJKER, H. & FRIJDA, N., 1960, *National Character and National Stereotypes*. Amsterdam: North Holland Publishing Co.

Education for All, 1985 (the Swann Report). London: H.M.S.O.

EDWARDS, A.D. & FURLONG, V.J., 1978, *The Language of Teaching*. London: Heinemann.

EDWARDS, J.R., 1977, Ethnic identity and bilingual education. In H. GILES (ed.), *Language Ethnicity and Intergroup Relations*, 253–82. London: Academic Press.

EHNERT, R., LONDEIX, F., ROBERTS, M. & RUTHERFORD, R., 1981, Essen und Trinken als Thema einer kontrastiven Landeskunde. *Bielefelder Beiträge für Sprachlehrforschung* 1, 74–109.

ELLIS, R., 1985, *Understanding Second Language Acquisition*. Oxford: O.U.P.

ESMAN, M.J., 1977, *Ethnic Conflict in the Western World*. Ithaca: Cornwall U.P.

FARR, R.M. & MOSCOVICI, S. (eds), 1984, *Social Representations*. Cambridge: C.U.P.

FIRGES, J. & MELENK, H., 1982, Landeskunde als Alltagswissen. *Praxis des neusprachlichen Unterrichts* 29, 2, 115–23.

FORTES, M., 1970, Social and psychological aspects of education in Taleland. In J. MIDDLETON (ed.), *From Child to Adult: Studies in the Anthropology of Education*. New York: Natural History Press.

FURNHAM, A. & BOCHNER, S. 1986, *Culture Shock, Psychological Reactions to Unfamiliar Environments*. London: Methuen.

GADOFFRE, G., 1951, French national images and the problem of national stereotypes. *International Social Science Bulletin* 3, 579–87.

GARDNER, R.C., 1985, *Social Psychology and Second Language Learning*. London: Arnold.

GEERTZ, C., 1975, *The Interpretation of Cultures*. London: Hutchinson.

GILBERT, M., 1953–5, The origins of the reform movement in modern language teaching in England. *Research Review* 4, 1–9; 5, 9–18; 6, 1–10.

GILES, H. & POWESLAND, P., 1975, *Speech Style and Social Evaluation*. London: Academic Press.

GOHRING, H., 1975, Kontrastive Kulturanalyse and Deutsch als Fremdsprache. *Jahrbuch Deutsch als Fremdsprache* 1, 80–92.

GOLDMANN, L., 1956, *Le Dieu Caché*. Paris: Gallimard.

GOODENOUGH, W.H., 1964, Cultural anthropology and linguistics. In D. HYMES (ed.), *Language in Culture and Society*. New York: Harper and Row.

GOODSON, I.F. & McGIVNEY, V., 1985, *European Dimensions and the Secondary School Curriculum*. Brighton: Falmer.

GRAS, S. & GRAS, C., 1982, *La révolte des régions d'Europe occidentale de 1916 à nos jours*. Paris: Presses universitaires de France.

GRINDHAMMER, L., 1978, 'Language learning and language teaching: the cultural imperative. *Anglistik und Englischunterricht* 4, Mai, 63–83.

GUDYKUNST, W.B. (ed.), 1986, *Intergroup Communication*. London: Edward Arnold.

GUTHRIE, G.P. & HALL, W.S., 1981, Introduction. In H.T. TRUEBA *et al.*, *Culture and the Bilingual Classroom*. Rowley, Mass: Newbury House.

HAARMANN, H., 1986, *Language in Ethnicity*. Berlin: Mouton de Gruyter.

HAAS, R. & SCHREY, H., 1983, Zum Stand der England- und Amerikakunde, *Die Neueren Sprachen*, 82, 5/6, 394–408.

HADLEY, C.G., 1983, Goffs School 'Section Bilingue'; mimeo.

HALL, E.T., 1959, *The Silent Language*. New York: Doubleday.

HAMERS, J. & BLANC, M., 1982, Cultural identity and bilinguality. In R.T. NOOR *et al.* (eds), *Foreign Language Teaching and Cultural Identity*. Brussels: AIMAV.

——1983, *Bilingualité et Bilinguisme*. Brussels: Pierre Mardaga.

HARNISCH, J.H., 1976, Der Fremdsprachenunterricht seit 1945: Geschichte und Ideologie. In J. KRAMER (ed.), *Bestandaufnahme Fremdsprachenunterricht*. Stuttgart: Metzler.

HAWKINS, E.W., 1981, *Modern Languages in the Curriculum*. Cambridge: C.U.P.

——1987, *Awareness of Language*, 2nd edn. Cambridge C.U.P.

H.M.I., 1977, *Curriculum 11–16*. London: H.M.S.O.

——1985, *The Curriculum from 5–16*. London: H.M.S.O.

——1987, *Modern Foreign Languages to 16*. London: H.M.S.O.

HOGGART, R., 1957, *The Uses of Literacy*. London: Chatto and Windus.

HOLLAND, D.C., 1985, From situation to impression: how Americans get to know themselves and one another. In J.W.D. DOUGHERTY (ed.), *Directions in Cognitive Anthropology*. Urbana: University of Illinois Press.

HOOPS, W., 1982, Sachtexte und ihre didaktischen Dimensionen. *Die Neueren Sprachen* 81, 2, 173–91.

HOUGH, G., 1966, *An Essay on Criticism*. London: Duckworth.

HSU, F.L.K., 1969, *The Study of Literate Civilisations*. New York: Holt Rinehart and Winston.

HUDSON, R.A., 1981, Some issues on which linguists can agree. *Journal of Linguistics* 17, 333–43.

HUHN, P., 1978, Landeskunde im Lehrbuch: Aspekte der Analyse, Kritik und korrektiven Behandlung. In W. KUHLWEIN & G. RADDEN (eds), *Sprache und Kultur*. Tübingen: Gunter Narr.

HUMPHREY, C.A., 1978, The role of Landeskunde in the academic training of German teachers of English. *Anglistik und Englischunterricht* 4, Mai, 9–14.

154   CULTURAL STUDIES IN FOREIGN LANGUAGE EDUCATION

HUNDEIDE, K., 1985, The tacit background of children's judgements. In J.W. WERTSCH (ed.), *Culture, Communication and Cognition*. Cambridge: C.U.P.

HURMAN, A., 1977, *As Others See Us*. London: Arnold.

HYMES, D.H., 1972, On Communicative Competence. In J.B. PRIDE & J. HOLMES (eds), *Sociolinguistics*. Harmondsworth: Penguin.

JENKINS, R., 1985, Ready for a marriage of academic convenience. *Times Higher Education Supplement*, 20 December.

JOINER, E.G., 1976, Evaluating the cultural context of foreign language texts. *Modern Languages Journal* 58, 242–44.

KACOWSKY, W., 1973, Stellung und Problematik der Kulturkunde im Fremdsprachenunterricht von heute. *Moderne Sprachen* 17, 1/2, 4–24.

KAPLAN, D. & MANNERS, R.A., 1972, *Culture Theory*. Englewood Cliffs, N.J.: Prentice Hall.

KELLER, G., 1978, Werden Vorurteile durch einen Schüleraustausch abgebaut? In H. ARNDT & F.R. WELLER (eds), *Landeskunde und Fremdsprachenunterricht*. Frankfurt a.m.: Diesterweg.

——1979, Die Auswirkungen eines Deutschlandaufenthaltes auf das Deutschlandbild britischer Schüler. *Die Neueren Sprachen* 78, 3, 212–31.

——1983a, Grundlegung einer neuen Kulturkunde als Orientierungsrahmen für Lehrerausbildung und Unterrichtspraxis. *Neusprachliche Mitteilungen aus Wissenschaft und Praxis* 4, November, 200–9.

——1983b, Didaktische Analyse eines neuen kulturkundlichen Unterrichts auf lern- und soziopsychologischer Grundlage. In A. RAASCH *et al.* (eds), *Beiträge zur Landeskunde im Fremdsprachenunterricht*. Frankfurt a. M.: Diesterweg.

KERL, D., 1979, Quo vadis, Landeskunde? *Zeitschrift für Anglistik und Amerikanistik* 27, 154–61.

KING, A., 1975, Sections bilingues in Somerset. *Modern Languages in Scotland* 6, 52–57.

KLEIN, W., 1986, *Second Language Acquisition*. Cambridge: C.U.P.

KNOX, E., 1982, Propos d'un usager. *Études de Linguistique Appliquée* 47, 8–20.

KOHRING, K.H. & SCHWERDTFEGER, I.C., 1976, Landeskunde im Fremdsprachenunterricht: eine Neubegründung unter semiotischem Aspekt. *Linguistik und Didaktik* 25, 55–80.

KRAMER, J., 1976, Cultural Studies versus Landes-/Kulturkunde. In J. KRAMER (ed.), *Bestandsaufnahme Fremdsprachenunterricht*. Stuttgart: Metzler.

KRUGER, M., 1981, Landeskundliche Inhalte: Lehrbuchanalyse und Planungskriterien. *Zielsprache Deutsch* 2, 26–32.

KRUMM, H.J., 1975, Kriterien zur Bewertung von Lehrwerken für den

Unterrichtsbereich Deutsch als Fremsprache. *Jahrbuch Deutsch als Fremdsprache* 1, 93–101.

LADO, R., 1957, *Linguistics across Cultures*. Ann Arbor: University of Michigan Press.

LAMBERT, W.E., 1974, An alternative to the foreign language teaching profession. In H.B. ALTMAN & V.E. HANZELI (eds), *Essays on the Teaching of Culture*. Detroit: Advancement Press of America.

——1977, The effects of bilingualism on the individual: cognitive and socio-cultural consequences. In P.A. HORNBY (ed.), *Bilingualism: Psychological, Social and Educational Implications*. New York: Academic Press.

——1978, Cognitive and socio-cultural consequences of bilingualism. *Canadian Modern Language Review* 34, 3, 537–47.

LAMBERT, W.E. & KLINEBERG, O., 1967, *Children's Views of Foreign Pupils*. New York: Appleton-Century-Crofts.

LEACH, E., 1982, *Social Anthropology*. Glasgow: Fontana.

LITTLEWOOD, W., 1981, *Communicative Language Teaching*. Cambridge: C.U.P.

——1984, *Foreign and Second Language Learning*. Cambridge: C.U.P.

LOVEDAY, L., 1982, *The Sociolinguistics of Learning and Using a Nonnative Language*. Oxford: Pergamon.

MACOS, 1968–70, *Man: a Course of Study*. Cambridge, Mass: Education Development Center.

MARIET, F. 1982, La formation d'une inculture, *Études de Linguistique Appliquée*, 47, 97–120.

——1985, La presse française telle que la connaissent et l'ignorent les étudiants en français aux États-Unis. *The French Review* 49, 2, 219–33.

MARLAND, M., 1986, Towards a curriculum policy for a multilingual world. *British Journal of Language Teaching* 24, 3, 123–38.

MARQUEZ, E.J., 1979, Contrastive analysis in sociolinguistics. *International Review of Applied Linguistics* 77, 3, 313–29.

MIDGLEY, M., 1980, *Beast and Man. The Roots of Human Nature*. London: Methuen.

MITCHELL, R., PARKINSON, B. & JOHNSTONE, R., 1981, *The Foreign Language Classroom: an observational study*. Stirling: University of Stirling.

MOSCOVICI, S., 1984, The phenomenon of social representations. In R.M. FARR & S. MOSCOVICI (eds), *Social Representations*. Cambridge: C.U.P.

MÜLLER, B.-D., 1980, Zur Logik interkultureller Verstehensprobleme. *Jahrbuch Deutsch als Fremdsprache* 6, 102–19.

NANDY, M., 1981, Social studies for a multiracial society. In A. JAMES &

R. JEFFCOATE (eds), *The School in the Multicultural Society*. London: Harper and Row.

NEWBY, M., 1981, *Making Language*. London: O.U.P.

OBLER, L.K., 1983, Knowledge in neurolinguistics: the case of bilingualism. *Language Learning* 33, 5, 159–91.

OCHS, E. & SCHIEFFELIN, B.B., 1984, Language acquisition and socialisation: three developmental stories and their implications. In R.A. SHWEDER & R.A. LEVINE (eds), *Culture Theory*. Cambridge: C.U.P.

OKSAAR, E., 1983, Language learning as cultural learning. *Rassegna Italiana di Linguistica Applicationa* 15, 2/3, 121–30.

PICHT, R. (ed.), 1975, *Deutschlandstudien Bd 1*. Bonn: D.A.A.D.

POIRIER, F. & ROSSELIN, M., 1982, Civiliser l'enseignement. *Langues Modernes* 76, 2, 177–88.

PORCHER, L., 1982, L'enseignement de la civilisation en question. *Études de Linguistique Appliquée* 47, 39–49.

QUINN, N., 1985, 'Commitment' in American marriage: on cultural analysis. In J.W.D. DOUGHERTY (ed.), *Directions in Cognitive Anthropology*. Urbana: University of Illinois Press.

RADDATZ, V., 1977, *Englandkunde im Wandel deutscher Erziehungsziele*. Königstein: Scriptor.

RICHARDS, J.C., 1982, Talking across cultures. *Language Learning and Communication* 1, 1, 61–71.

RILEY, P., 1981, Towards a contrastive pragmatics. In J. FISIAK (ed.), *Contrastive Linguistics and the Language Teacher*. Oxford: Pergamon.

——1984, Understanding misunderstandings: cross-cultural pragmatic failure in the language classroom. *European Journal of Teacher Education* 7, 2, 127–44.

RISAGER, K. & ANDERSEN, H., 1978, Forholdet mellem sprogligt og samfundsmaessigt indhold: fremmedsprogsundervisningen. *TRUC: Tidsskrift for Romansk ved Universitetscentrene*. Roskilde: R.U.C.

RUMELHART, D.E., 1980, Schemata: the building blocks of cognition. In R.J. SPIRO *et al.* (eds), *Theoretical Issues in Reading Comprehension*. Hillsdale, N.J.: Lawrence Erlbaum Associates.

SCHANK, R.C. & ABELSON, R.R., 1977, *Scripts, Plans, Goals and Understanding*. Hillsdale, N.J.: Lawrence Erlbaum Associates.

SCHOOLS COUNCIL, 1981, *Graded Objectives and Tests for Modern Languages: an Evaluation*. London: Schools Council.

SCHREY, H., 1982, *Anglistisches Kaleidoskop*. Sankt Augustin: Hans Richarz.

SCHUMANN, J.H., 1978, Social and psychological factors in second language acquisition. In J.C. RICHARDS (ed.), *Understanding Second and Foreign Language Learning*. Rowley, Mass: Newbury House.

SEELYE, H.N., 1974, *Teaching Culture*. Skokie, Ill: National Textbook Co.

SHWEDER, R.A. & LEVINE, R.A., 1984, *Culture Theory*. Cambridge: C.U.P.

SIDWELL, D., 1984, *Teaching Languages to Adults*. London: C.I.L.T.

SPERBER, D., 1985, *On Anthropological Knowledge*. Cambridge: C.U.P.

SPICER, A. & RIDDY, D.C., 1977, *Initial Training and Teachers of Modern Languages*. Leeds: E.J. Arnold.

STAUBLE, A.-M. E., 1980, Acculturation and second language acquisition. In R. SCARCELLA & S.D. KRASHEN (eds), *Research in Second Language Acquisition*. Rowley, Mass: Newbury House.

STENHOUSE, L., 1975, *An Introduction to Curriculum Research and Development*. London: Heinemann.

STUBBS, M.W., 1983, *Language, Schools and Classrooms* (2nd edn). London: Methuen.

SWAIN, M. & LAPKIN, S., 1982, *Evaluating Bilingual Education: A Canadian Case Study*. Clevedon, Avon: Multilingual Matters.

TAYLOR, C., 1971, Interpretation and the sciences of man. *The Review of Metaphysics* 25, 1, 3–51.

THOMAS, J., 1983, Cross-cultural pragmatic failure. *Applied Linguistics* 4, 2, 91–112.

TOSI, A., 1986, Home and community language teaching for bilingual learners: issues in planning and instruction. *Language Teaching* 19, 1, 2–23.

TRIANDIS, H.C., 1972, *The Analysis of Subjective Culture*. New York: John Wiley.

——1975, Culture training, cognitive complexity and interpersonal attitudes. In R.W. BRISLIN *et al.* (eds), *Cross-Cultural Perspectives on Learning*. New York: John Wiley.

TRIANDIS, H.C. & LAMBERT, W.W., 1980, *Handbook of Cross-Cultural Psychology*, Vol. 1. Boston: Allyn and Bacon.

TRIM, J.L.M., 1980, Progress towards a more comprehensive framework for the definition of language learning objectives. *Modern Languages (1971–1981)*. Strasbourg: Council of Europe.

——1983, 'Yes, but what do you mean by "communication"?' In C. BRUMFIT (ed.), *Learning and Teaching Languages for Communication: Applied Linguistic Perspectives*. London: C.I.L.T.

UHLEMANN, H., 1979, Das Lehrfach Landeskunde in seiner Beziehung zur Kommunikativen Zielstellung des Deutschunterrichts. *Deutsch als Fremdsprache* 16, 225–34.

VALDES, J.M. (ed.) 1986, *Culture Bound. Bridging the cultural gap in language teaching*. Cambridge: C.U.P.

VALDMAN, A., 1966, *Trends in Language Teaching*. London: McGraw Hill.

158   CULTURAL STUDIES IN FOREIGN LANGUAGE EDUCATION

VAN ELS, T., 1982, De Bellagio Declaration. *Levende Talen* 374, 597–99.
VISAGE, J., 1982, Choisir des documents pour un cours de langue et civilisation. *Études de Linguistique Appliquée* 47, 30–38.
VON WRIGHT, G.H., 1971, *Explanation and Understanding*. London: Routledge & Kegan Paul.
VYGOTSKY, L.S., 1971, *Mind in Society*. Cambridge, Mass: Harvard University Press.
WAX, R., 1971, *Doing Fieldwork*. Chicago: University of Chicago Press.
WEIL, R., 1982, The training of teachers of modern languages in England and France. In R. GOODINGS, M. BYRAM & M. MCPARTLAND (eds), *Changing Priorities in Teacher Education*. London: Croom Helm.
WELLS, G., 1987, *The Meaning Makers*. London: Hodder and Stoughton.
WERTSCH, J.V. & STONE, C.A., 1985, The concept of internalization in Vygotsky's account of the genesis of higher mental functions. In J.V. WERTSCH (ed.), *Culture, Communication and Cognition*. Cambridge: C.U.P.
WIDDOWSON, H., 1985, Comprehension as negotiation: a consideration of general issues. In R. EPPENEDER (ed.), *Comprehension as Negotiation of Meaning*. Munich: Goethe Institut.
WILLIAMS, R., 1965, *The Long Revolution*. Harmondsworth: Penguin.
WILLIAMS, T.R., 1967, *Field Methods in the Study of Culture*. New York: Holt Rinehart and Winston.
WINCH, P., 1964, Understanding a primitive society. *American Philosophical Quarterly* 1, 4, 307–24.
WYLIE, L., (ed.) 1966, *Chanzeaux. A village in Anjou*. Cambridge, Mass: Harvard University Press.
ZARATE, G., 1986, *Enseigner une Culture Étrangère*. Paris: Hachette.
ZIEGESAR, D., 1978, 'Popular culture' im Fremdsprachenunterricht der Sekundarstufe 2 und im Hochschulbereich. *Anglistik und Englischunterricht* 4 (May), 103–24.

Index